Wonder
and
Critical Reflection

An Invitation to Philosophy

Tom Christenson
Capital University

UPPER SADDLE RIVER, NEW JERSEY 07458

Library of Congress Cataloging-in-Publication Data

CHRISTENSON, TOM.
  Wonder and critical reflection: an invitation to philosophy / TOM CHRISTENSON.
    p. cm.
  Includes bibliographical references and index.
  ISBN 0-13-040041-6
    1. Philosophy—Introductions. I. Title.
  BD21.C558   2001
  100—dc21   00-059832

This book is dedicated to my children:
Nick, Maren, Elise, Forest, and Zoe,
wonderers all.

VP, Editorial Director: *Charlyce Jones Owen*
Acquisitions Editor: *Ross Miller*
Editorial Assistant : *Carla Worner*
Editorial/Production Supervision: *Edie Riker*
Prepress and Manufacturing Buyer: *Sherry Lewis*
Marketing Manager: *Don Allmon*
Cover Director: *Jayne Conte*
Cover Designer: *Bruce Kenselaar*

This book was set in 10/12 Stone Serif by East End Publishing Services, Inc., and was printed and bound by Courier Companies, Inc. The cover was printed by Phoenix Color Corp.

© 2001 by Prentice-Hall, Inc.
A Division of Pearson Education
Upper Saddle River, New Jersey 07458

Printed in the United States of America

10   9   8   7   6   5   4   3   2   1

ISBN   0-13-040041-6

Prentice-Hall International (UK) Limited, *London*
Prentice-Hall of Australia Pty. Limited, *Sydney*
Prentice-Hall Canada Inc., *Toronto*
Prentice-Hall Hispanoamericana, S.A., *Mexico*
Prentice-Hall of India Private Limited, *New Delhi*
Prentice-Hall of Japan, Inc., *Tokyo*
Pearson Education Asia Pte. Ltd., *Singapore*
Editora Prentice-Hall do Brasil, Ltda., *Rio de Janeiro*

Contents

CHAPTER TWO

Three Common Temptations, 17

CHAPTER THREE

Philosophy as Cultural Criticism, 27

CHAPTER FOUR

Philosophy as Cultural Conservation, 43

CHAPTER FIVE
Philosophy and the Labyrinth of Language, 55

CHAPTER SIX
Freedom and Self-Determination, 69

CHAPTER SEVEN
The Search for the Authentic Self, 87

CHAPTER EIGHT

Questions, Questions, and More Questions! 107

Preface

Philosophy is disciplined critical reflection (about fundamental ideas) that springs from wonder. In the process of this book we will unpack this definition, attempting to explain as well as illustrate what it means for philosophy to be disciplined, for it to be critical reflection, what fundamental ideas are, and what it means for philosophy to spring from wonder.

Beginning students very often find philosophy puzzling and more than a little bit peculiar. Here are three quotes from student essays that express some of that peculiarity:

> Philosophy requires an open mind. People who are afraid to ask themselves hard questions seem turned off by it. It makes you think past "the usual answers," and sometimes we don't want to do that.

> Most of the things you learn in college teach you the right answers. Philosophy is not like that—it leaves you with many more questions than when you came in—and the problem is they are deep, troublesome questions, the kind that continue to bother you long after the course is done.

> It's common enough that we speak in clichés. But I discovered through studying philosophy how often we also think in them

and even perceive the world in clichéd ways. Philosophy is a way
to make us realize this and to help us get beyond it.

Philosophy is a peculiar enterprise in more than one way. It requires
a peculiar sort of person to do it, it has peculiar temptations for those
who engage in it, and it requires a difficult kind of balancing between
extremes in order to be done well. This peculiarity is what makes philosophy interesting, challenging, and fun. I invite you to try it.

Chapters One and Two of this book try to explain what philosophy is, who would be interested in doing it, and what some of the common temptations are for those who pursue it. Chapters Three and Four
explore the ways in which philosophy is critical of culture and the ways
in which it is culturally conservative. Chapter Four also includes examples of three contemporary thinkers who embody both of these aspects
of philosophy. Chapter Five explores the problems that we run into
with language and the ways philosophers try to identify and avoid
these problems. Chapters Six and Seven are discussions of two particular philosophical issues, freedom and human nature/selfhood. Chapter
Seven explores the works of several provocative thinkers on these topics. Chapter Eight returns to the general topic of the nature of philosophy and examines why philosophical inquiries often generate more
questions than definitive answers. Is this a sign of philosophy's failure
or a sign of its success?

The purpose of this book is not to tell you *about* philosophy,
although you can learn some things about philosophy and philosophers from reading it. Its main purpose is *to invite and provoke you to
engage in philosophical thinking*, to experience firsthand the wonder, the
temptations, the critical tools, and the pleasure of it. This is why it is
designed in an open-textured way, including dialogues, explanations,
discussions, and questions in each of the chapters. The book will be
successful if you are provoked to wonder and to reflect critically by the
discussions initiated in it. This book does not pretend to offer a complete discussion of any of the topics it raises, but rather should be used
as a place for a continuing discussion to begin. The questions that follow each chapter are designed to engage you in such a discussion,
which is, after all, what philosophy really is.

CHAPTER ONE

The Idea of Philosophy

This chapter begins with a dialogue that explores some preconceptions and stereotypes and invites us to consider why we so often think in terms of them. The discussion looks at the original meaning of "philosophy" and attempts a contemporary translation of the idea. We then explore the kinds of questions philosophy raises and their connection to experiences of wonder.

Dialogue I

Ryan: Your name is Sarah, right? I'm Ryan.

Sarah: Hi!

R: I guess we're stuck in this class together. Are you majoring in economics?

S: No, I'm just taking the class because I'm interested.

R: So what is your major?

S: I'm a little undecided, but I think it will be philosophy.

R: Oh. —

S: What's the matter? Does that answer end the conversation?

R: Yeah—I mean no. Uh—that's pretty—uh—heavy stuff.

S: C'mon, say what you're thinking.

R: Well, it's kind of weird. You don't seem typical.

S: Gee! Is that supposed to be a compliment or what? Do you mean philosophy is weird, or it's weird that I'm studying it?

R: Both, I guess.

S: Explain what you mean.

R: People who study philosophy are sort of—radical, you know what I mean?

S: No, I don't. Do you know some other people who are majoring in philosophy?

R: No, I guess you're the first one I've really met.

S: But still you have a clear idea of what a typical philosophy major is like?

R: Yeah, I guess I do.

S: So what is this idea?

R: Well, a female philosophy major would typically be a radical feminist. You know, someone who doesn't wear makeup, doesn't shave her legs, looks kind of dumpy, maybe is a lesbian.

S: If you've never met a female philosophy major before, where did you get such an impression?

R: I don't know; it's the sort of thing you hear.

S: And since it's the "sort of thing you hear" it must be true, right? Isn't that what you're assuming?

R: I guess so; I mean, why would people say it if it weren't so?

S: That's a good question. Why do people think in stereotypes? There's the stereotypical football player, the stereotypical accountant, math major, librarian, attorney, etc. Do you believe all these stereotypes?

R: I don't know. It just makes it easier to get along. Without stereo-types lots of jokes wouldn't make sense—like stereotypical salesmen, blacks, Jews, blondes, gays, cops, etc.

S: Aren't stereotypes ways of avoiding dealing with individual people? You just lump them in some category, make a judgment of them on the basis of that, and then you don't have to deal with them any further.

R: Well, what the heck. Why make such a big deal about it?

S: The big deal is that stereotypes reinforce a kind of prejudice, and prejudice can do a lot of harm. There are two other philosophy majors in this class, but I bet you can't tell which students they are.

R: So?

S: So that shows what your stereotype is worth.

R: Just forget it.

S: Forget what?

R: Well, when I first introduced myself I was thinking about asking you out.

S: But when you heard I was a philosophy major you had second thoughts?

R: Yeah.

S: And now you definitely don't want to ask me out because you don't like women who take ideas seriously and think critically?

R: You've got that right.

S: Well, so long. At least I learned something from this conversation.

R: Aren't you even going to ask me what my major is?

S: No.

R: Why not?

S: I don't want to form a negative stereotype.

Philosophy: What Is It?

Most students coming to college have a fairly good idea what biology, chemistry, history, and political science are. They may be slightly less clear about studies such as physics, psychology, sociology, theology, and musicology. But my experience is that very few arrive in college knowing what philosophy is. This is true in spite of the fact that philos-ophy is not some new field of study. It is, in fact, one of the oldest dis-ciplines around, predating all those just listed with perhaps one exception. So it is not at all unusual for students reading over a sched-ule of courses to raise the question, "What is philosophy?" That's the question we want to try to answer by looking briefly at the discipline's history, by discussing the kinds of inquiries it pursues, and, finally and most importantly, by doing it.

Philosophy: The Word and the Idea

The word "philosophy" is Greek in origin. It is a composite of two Greek roots: *philein,* one of the Greek words for love, and *sophia,* the Greek word for wisdom. Combined they mean "the love or pursuit of wisdom." From the very beginning in the fifth century B.C.E., people who used the word seemed to wish to make a distinction by using it: between *those who claimed to be wise*—sophists, and *those who, although not claiming wisdom, still loved it and pursued it*—philosophers.

In some ways "wisdom" is an old-fashioned word. We seldom hear people talk about wisdom except in mottos or insignias of universities. Just about the only time we use the term in everyday discourse we use it sarcastically, as in "Well, ain't you the wise guy." We sometimes talk about wise decisions or wise investments, but seldom talk about people being wise or pursuing wisdom. Wisdom is not valued by most of us in the way it once was. Occasionally someone will bring it to mind as an ideal that we have lost sight of. How, then, can it make sense to contemporary students that wisdom should be pursued?

Perhaps the most helpful thing to do is to translate the idea into a more contemporary idiom. The problem is that no single word in English is the exact equivalent of "wisdom." The closest we can come may be to suggest that it is the combination of several ideas. **Philosophy is disciplined critical reflection (about fundamental ideas) that springs from wonder.** The sections that follow attempt to explain what kinds of things fundamental ideas are, and what critical reflection looks like, so we will say no more about that right now. But first a clarifying word about wonder and its connection to philosophy is necessary before we proceed further.

Philosophy and Wonder

From philosophy's beginnings in ancient Greece, thinkers asserted the connection between philosophy and wonder. Plato wrote, "Wonder is the feeling of a philosopher, and philosophy is rooted in wonder" (*Theatetus*, 155d.) Aristotle reiterated his teacher's point: "For it is owing to their wonder that people both now begin and at first began to philosophize" (*Metaphysics*, 12, 982b.) So what is the connection

Socrates, Plato, and Aristotle

Between 469 and 322 B.C.E., the Greek city-state Athens was home to three of the most original and influential thinkers in the Western philosophical tradition. **Socrates** (469–399), although he never established any "school," daily discussed philosophical issues in the public places of Athens. **Plato** (428–347) was one of the young Athenians who took an interest and so, in a sense, became one of Socrates' "students." Plato, later in his career, began a school in Athens, the Academy, which enrolled yet another brilliant student, **Aristotle** (384–322).

Although Socrates wrote no philosophical works himself, Plato memorialized his teacher by writing many dialogues that featured Socrates discussing a variety of philosophical issues, for example, on the nature of courage, piety, friendship, justice, and the immortality of the soul. Some of these dialogues arise as chance encounters in the streets of Athens; some occur as discussions at dinner parties or at the homes of friends and acquaintances. One of them, *The Phaedo*, is even set in a prison cell on the day of Socrates' execution. *The Apology* gives an account of the trial that led to Socrates' conviction and sentencing.

The works of Aristotle come to us as tightly constructed and thoroughly argued essays on a great variety of topics including ethics, politics, the nature of the soul, logic, the basic structure of reality, and the art of tragic drama. At one point in his career Aristotle was private tutor to the son of King Phillip of Macedon. The lad later came to be the ruler of the entire Mediterranean world, Alexander the Great. Eventually Aristotle returned to Athens and established his own school, the Lyceum.

The writings of Plato and Aristotle set the agenda for philosophical thinking in the Western world from their day to our own. A.N. Whitehead commented that the history of Western thought can be seen as "a series of footnotes to Plato."

between philosophy and wonder? Why is it still important to emphasize this connection?

What is wonder? Wonder is a response we find ourselves making to things that amaze us, awe us, bewilder us, puzzle us, and shock us into a new state of awareness and new patterns of thinking. Wonder usually occurs not the first time we experience something, but the first time we really see what we have looked at a thousand times but have never stopped to notice before. Wonder occurs experientially but can also occur conceptually, when we understand (or see that we do not understand) something in a new way. Wonder is the experience of the familiar as suddenly unfamiliar, the encounter with the usual in a way that suddenly makes it shockingly new and fresh.

An acquaintance of mine related to me the following experience when I asked him about experiences of wonder:

> The winter of my eighth grade year I purchased and built a refractor telescope from a kit. It was not very powerful. An excellent pair of binoculars purchased nowadays would probably outperform it. I built a tripod and a mount from stuff in our basement. By Christmas of that year I was ready to take it out to see how it would perform. The skies in northern Minnesota in midwinter tend to be crystal clear unless it's snowing. Many nights I stood outside in our backyard, peering through the eyepiece trying to find planets and star clusters and get them focused for viewing. Almost every night I would stay out until my feet became completely numb, then I'd come in, warm up for a bit, and then go out again for another bout with the deep black sky and the numbing cold. The telescope certainly had its problems; the mount and tripod I built had several design and execution flaws as well. Then there was the human error of aiming, or once finding the celestial object of holding the scope still while I adjusted the focus knob with my frozen fingers. But in spite of fallible tools, fierce conditions, and my own voluminous ignorance, I had a great time. My mother was concerned, not only for my physical health but my mental well-being as well. What kind of kid would stand out in that subzero cold to peer at the stars? Not a normal one for sure.

> I remember seeing the moons of Jupiter as they shifted slightly night after night, getting a sense of the three-dimensionality of their orbits as they performed their dance in front of a backdrop of more distant stars. I knew enough to know what a light-year was, and that the light from many of the stars I saw had issued from them thousands, perhaps millions, of years before. I realized in a very unsophisticated way that I was seeing not only into distant space but also into distant time. I wondered whether the things I saw were still there, shedding that same light into the great vastness of which I was also a part. I imagined the infinity of space and found it inconceivable. I imagined the finitude of space and found it just as inconceivable. I imagined the infinite smallness and unimportance of my world compared to what I was seeing and found it inconceivable. I considered that

my world might be the measure and the meaning of all I saw and I considered that equally inconceivable. I found that the more I found out about the planetary system, our galaxy and the deep space of other galaxies the more amazed I was. I stood out there watching and wondering in the cold, not just because of what I saw, which was certainly wondrous enough, but also because of what I knew, imagined, and found myself incapable of imagining.

Wonder is not a function of sophisticated equipment, nor is it a function of how much you know. Wonder can be experienced by an ordinary person observing something as common as a dandelion. But, contrary to the beliefs of some romantics, wonder is not a function of how little we know either. Many practicing scientists pursue their studies of galaxies, the mating patterns of geese, cures for diseases, and geologic structures in wonder-filled ways.

Instead of being a function of knowledge or ignorance, wonder seems to be a function of openness. It has more to do with our attitude and orientation to things rather than the degree of our knowledge or ignorance. Wonder is the opposite of narrow-mindedness, of looking at things only in the accustomed way. Wonder is the opposite of banality, complacency, and boredom. It's the sort of thing one can gain, lose, regain, nurture, and cultivate. Wonder is not something that can be strictly taught, although it certainly can be expressed, and in that sense shared and sometimes engendered and enabled in others.

Some poetry, at least, is the expression of wonder found in the most ordinary places. Here's an example of a poem written by William Carlos Williams, one of America's most famous poets. He was also a physician who worked in Paterson, New Jersey:

BETWEEN WALLS
the back wings
of the

hospital where
nothing

will grow lie
cinders

in which shine
the broken

pieces of a green
bottle

Williams does not romanticize the broken bottle, nor the cinders, nor the rear of the hospital. He records them in a very plain way, celebrating their plainness, their ordinariness, their castawayness. Still he is able to show us, by the way he attends to them and fashions his simple fragments of verse, that they are a place of wonder.

Philosophy, like poetry, can be important for the fresh-eyed approach it brings to things. When something gets to be too routine, or when an inquiry becomes simply the repeated application of some formulaic method, or when everybody thinks "the answer is obvious," or when we have all become too complacent in our ways of doing and looking at things, then someone needs to show up who will pose the embarrassing question, who will crack the mold and question the assumptions everybody has been working with.

Questions are the tools of philosophy in the way that verse is the tool of poets. Each generation must relearn to pose the mold-cracking and eye-opening questions. This isn't possible without being wonder awake. Philosophy, without wonder, can itself become doctrinaire, authoritarian, and scholastic. It can become merely the learning of a whole bunch of "isms." Genuine philosophy is not merely the passing along of the wisdom of the past, but learning again to ask the kinds of questions that wise people in the past knew how to ask. It is learning to see once again with the inquiring eyes they knew how to see with.

So wonder is not just the place where philosophy began, nor is it just a kind of curiosity that is satisfied once understanding comes. Wonder is the continuing attitude of the philosopher. It makes one willing "to open the inquiry again from the beginning and rethink things from their foundations," as Plato records Socrates stating toward the end of many of his philosophical discourses. To proceed without abiding wonder is one of the perennial temptations of philosophy, but also, as we will see, its ruination. Without continuing wonder, philosophy turns into something else altogether.

Who Is Likely to Become a Philosopher?

Philosophers, like poets, can come from anywhere; philosophy is not profession specific. What is required is not so much a specific training, but rather a certain way of looking at and questioning things. I know philosophers who are farmers, bankers, insurance executives, journalists, medical doctors, biologists, physicists, religious leaders, and teachers of just about any discipline one can mention. Many of them, of course, might find it strange to think of themselves as philosophers. That's OK. What's required is a particular way of asking questions,

Iris Murdoch, 1910–1999

Irish born and Oxford and Cambridge educated, Iris Murdoch is an example of an exceptional contemporary philosopher who made her living (at least during most of her adult life) doing something other than teaching philosophy. Although she has several philosophical books and essays to her credit, for example, *The Sovereignty of Good* (1970) and *Metaphysics as a Guide to Morals* (1992), she is mainly known as a prolific and widely read novelist. Some of the best known of her novels are *The Bell* (1958), *A Severed Head* (1963), *The Good Apprentice* (1985), *Message to the Planet* (1990) and *Jackson's Dilemma* (1995). Many of her novels pose profound philosophical questions, particularly about the nature of freedom and selfhood. Murdoch won the prestigious Booker Prize for English fiction in 1978.

questioning answers, and thinking things through. Many people do that whether they call themselves philosophers or not.

One of my teachers was the philosopher Paul Weiss. He told the following story:

My first day in elementary school we sat in a classroom that had all the letters of the alphabet printed on cards strung out across the room above the blackboard. The first thing the teacher said was, "Just think, boys and girls, every word in the English language can be written using just these twenty-six letters." I raised my hand and asked her to spell one word after another, trying to find one word that she could not spell with those letters. I didn't quit; she finally had to shut me up. At that point I should have known I was destined to be a philosopher. Why? Because: (1) I wouldn't accept things just because they were said by an authority. (2) I looked for counterexamples to every generalization that people made. (3) I didn't know until I was well into it that I had tackled a problem that was too big for me to handle.

My own first indication that I might be a philosopher did not occur until I was in high school. In a physics class the teacher was explaining Bernoulli's principle: a faster moving fluid (for example, air) will have a proportionally lower pressure than a slower moving or stationary fluid. This principle is evidenced by the fact that an airplane wing has lift, that it is possible to sail a sailboat into the wind, that smoke will go out the window of a moving car but may stay inside a standing one, and so on. After the physics teacher's presentation I asked, "So why does this happen?" The teacher responded, "It happens because of Bernoulli's principle." I thought about this for a moment and then I said, "But why is Bernoulli's principle true?" He answered, "Because a faster moving fluid has a lower pressure than a slower moving fluid." Then I asked, "And why is that the case?" He said, now becoming agitated, "Because of Bernoulli's principle." Finally I said, "What kind of answer is that? It seems to me it's not an answer at all but just a name we have given to our ignorance." He responded, "What are you, some kind of damn philosopher?" I shrugged my shoulders, not knowing at the time exactly what a philosopher was. But, as it turned out, he was right. A "damn philosopher" is what I was and have turned out to be, and I am proud of it.

A recent philosophy major told me that she came to the university thinking she might like to study both literature and economics. She began taking courses in both those areas but switched to philosophy because, as she said;

> The kinds of questions I found it interesting to think about were questions that occurred to me while studying literature and economics, what I would call the "big questions" about human life and its orientation and meaning and whether we know what we claim to know. But these questions I really wasn't encouraged to pursue in those disciplines. My English prof finally pointed out to me that these were philosophical questions and that maybe I should try a class in philosophy to see how I liked it. I did, and I discovered that this is where I belong because these are the kinds of questions I ask.

From these examples can we draw any conclusions about what characteristics someone might have in order to be a philosopher? Maybe a few. A philosopher will have (1) An abiding wonder, and a desire to ask questions combined with the recognition that she doesn't know the answer and/or that he doesn't really understand the "official answer" that has been offered. (2) A willingness to question authority, not in order to be disruptive but out of a genuine attempt to understand what lies at the heart of things. (3) A willingness to ask fundamental or "radical" questions, that is, radical in the sense of questions that probe at the roots (a radish is a root crop) of things, in the places that other people take for granted. (4) A willingness to be self-critical, to subject one's own thinking to the same critical standards that one demands of others.

The first characteristic, wonder, we already talked about briefly. The remaining three we expand on in the discussions that follow.

On the "Impoliteness" of Philosophy

A few semesters ago a student stopped after class to complain that she didn't like philosophy. I inquired why. She said, "Philosophy is so impolite. First of all we talk about things my parents said we shouldn't talk about—like politics and religion and our deepest beliefs. Second, we argue a lot of the time. My parents told us not to do that. They were always saying, 'Stop your arguing!' Third, you encourage us to criticize each other's views, but I don't think criticism is very nice." I thanked her for pointing out to me just how odd a philosophy class must seem to somebody encountering it for the first time. It looked to her like the sort of activity that nice polite people just wouldn't do.

Part of this student's problems with philosophy stemmed from some misunderstandings or misapplications of what her parents intended with their advice. My guess (and my hope) is that her parents were not telling her that subjects like politics and religion should never be discussed. They were probably suggesting that there are better and worse places to have such discussions, and certainly there are better and worse ways of pursuing such discussions. It is surely very impolite to ask someone about their deeply held beliefs only to begin attacking them or making fun of them. Such "discussions" seldom are productive of anything besides hurt feelings and resentment. But there are discussions where all the participants can learn something. I may learn something from having to articulate my viewpoint, and I may learn something from hearing others do so as well. From discussion I can learn the strong and weak points of my own and others' thinking. Moreover, in this process I can practice critical and creative thinking myself. When I am called to write or speak on a topic, I frequently will try to find someone who will discuss it with me. In the process of discussion I can clarify my own thinking as well as hear points of view I had not considered.

Arguing is *the process of giving reasons* for what we think. If you think doctor-assisted suicide should be made illegal, I will want to know why you think that. Giving your reasons is making an argument. The parents of the student just quoted were probably not requiring her to stop giving reasons or asking for reasons. That is a very worthwhile activity, and one of the very best ways to learn anything. What they were probably demanding is that she (and her brothers and sisters?) stop *quarreling*. Quarreling uses techniques (like whining, bullying, shouting, name-calling, etc.) that are completely out of place in argument. The point of argument is to make the process of thought and the relation between reasons and conclusions explicit. The point of quarreling is to demolish one's opponent, to make oneself look good at someone else's expense. Parents should take care what they say to their kids, lest they give arguing an undeservedly bad name.

The Honor of Being Criticized

One Sunday many years ago, I was invited to my wife's grandparents' home for Sunday dinner. The grandfather, in his eighties, had suffered a stroke several years before and was partially crippled. After dinner, as we sat around and talked, the grandfather made several racist remarks and slurs about other ethnic and religious groups. At first I said nothing, being new to the situation and a guest in the house. His family made no response to his remarks. But finally I spoke up and told him I thought his remarks were offensive, prejudiced, and based on caricatures of persons of specific races and religions. The other family members were shocked that I would criticize him in this way. After all, as they later explained away from his hearing, he was an old man and not someone to take seriously. Later in the day I helped carry him back to his bed. As I was lowering him onto his pillow, he grabbed my shirt with his one good hand and pulled me close to him. Then he said, "Thank you for taking me seriously enough to argue with me. Everybody else around here just thinks I'm an old fool." After that day the two of us became very good friends. He and I continued to talk and argue with each other with deep mutual respect. We didn't always agree, but we came to know that we could count on each other to say what we were really thinking.

When wouldn't we want to criticize someone's ideas? I can think of only a few situations. It wouldn't make sense to criticize someone if (1) the topic is too trivial to deserve criticism, (2) the person is too immature or feeble to understand what we are saying, (3) we believe the person to be incorrigible, (i.e. he or she is beyond learning anything or improving themselves from the criticism). So we can see from such a list that refusing to criticize my thinking is not a compliment paid to me. Criticizing my thinking, in fact, treats me with honor. It says to me that you think my ideas are important and I am rational and capable of learning. There is only one other case where criticism of my thinking would be inappropriate, and that is in case my thinking is infallible (i.e., never open to even the possibility of error). Although there are several people whose thinking I value and trust, I have never met anyone whose thinking is infallible. So I don't think we have to worry very much about that exception. The very best thinkers make mistakes and are happy to learn about it when they do.

The Kinds of Questions Philosophers Ask

Philosophy is not defined by a specific subject matter like biology or geology are. We can think philosophically about any subject matter. That's why philosophy has so many subfields: philosophy of religion, philosophy of art, philosophy of science, philosophy of education, and so on. Philosophy is defined instead by the kinds of questions that are pursued. Earlier we categorized these as fundamental or radical questions (i.e., questions that probe the foundations or roots of our thinking). In philosophy these questions usually fall into one of the following categories: questions about what our assertions mean, questions about what we know and the reasons for our beliefs, and questions about how to live.

Questions About Meaning

Philosophers are not glib users of language. Rather than just repeating what they have heard others say so frequently, philosophers are likely to stop and ask, "What does this mean? Do we really understand what we're talking about when we talk this way?" For example, we might wonder about the meaning of religious language. Is language about God primarily language that refers to an entity beyond our experience, or is it language that is primarily expressive of a sense of depth and reverence, or is it both of these, or something else entirely? When a priest or pastor is asked to give an invocation at some public gathering, what exactly is taking place? Is the person describing something that is true, prescribing a way of looking at things, realizing something in the attitude and orientation of those present, talking complete nonsense, or something else entirely? It should be clear from the examples given that answering such questions is not easy, not even for a person well acquainted with the language use in question. A pastor may never have inquired about what a peculiar use of language an invocation is, in spite of doing thousands of them. Familiarity in such a case may, in fact, make one less likely to wonder, not more. What, for another example, did my physics teacher mean by claiming that Bernoulli's principle *explained* the phenomena we were studying? What constitutes something as a scientific explanation? Is giving a name to a set of phenomena an explanation? Is that what he was doing? Do we know anything significant when we "know" that objects fall "because of gravity" or is this another "name for our ignorance"? How do scientific explanations explain?

Questions Regarding Knowledge and Belief

Philosophers frequently ask us to justify our claims to know what we claim to know. Do we really know why objects fall and have weight? Do we have good reasons to think that incest is morally wrong? If so, what are they? What is it we know when we know that? Do we know that nature is orderly, or is this something we assume whenever we pursue science? If we know it, what is our knowledge of this basic principle based on? Is it like knowledge we obtain from observation or is it quite different? Do we, in fact, know what our country's founding documents claim, that all people have "certain inalienable rights"? How would we support the claim to know such a thing? Is religious belief rational? What kinds of reasons support it? What kind of reasons challenge it?

Questions About How to Live

Philosophers have traditionally also thought about what it means to live a fulfilled, fully realized, responsible human life. They have theorized about and tried to live out their ideas about such issues: how life ought to be oriented, what things a good life should focus on, how we should optimally live together, how we should relate to nature, what characteristics we should strive to develop in ourselves and in the young through education, what kinds of institutions we need and what kind we would be better off without, what is the nature of moral evil. These issues are generally classified as questions of ethics, morality, political ideology, and sometimes as issues of public policy.

Philosophy and Fundamental Ideas

Some ideas, like those questioned earlier, lie at the very foundations of a good deal of our thinking; they are fundamental in the sense that we presuppose them when we think about other things. How many enterprises and institutions, for example, depend on the ideas of freedom and responsibility? Or consider the idea of human nature. What is it that all humans share that makes us human? Is it something we are born with, something we achieve or forfeit, something some of us can possess more completely than others? Or is there nothing we all share? Our entire legal system, our efforts at education, our ways of thinking about psychological problems and therapy, our ways of thinking about morality, as well as many concepts that arise in political and religious contexts, all of these seem to presuppose that we understand such basic, fundamental ideas. Do we?

All academic disciplines claim to produce some kind of knowledge. But what exactly is knowledge? Is it one thing or many very different things simply called by the same name? How is knowledge different from belief? When are claims to know something justified and when not? What is the difference, for example, between genuine medical practice and medical "quackery"? When is a person acting rationally and when not? When do we feel justified in institutionalizing someone because they are no longer rational or responsible? Theorizing about such ideas as freedom, responsibility, human nature, knowledge, and rationality is a very important activity. Trying to understand these fundamental ideas and give a coherent account of them is one of the principal tasks of philosophy.

Philosophy, over the centuries, has sprouted many subdisciplines as these inquiries have become specialized. Political theory, social theory, education theory, psychology and economic theory were, and to a large degree still are, a part of philosophy. As long as the inquiry is still essentially open, as long as it questions its fundamental ideas, as long as it springs from wonder, it is a part of philosophy. Where it has become an application of some predetermined methodology it usually becomes something else, a specialized subdiscipline focused on answering clearly bounded questions in a prescribed way. Philosophy occurs where the fundamental ideas, the method of inquiry, and the desired outcome are still open to question and debate. Philosophy occurs where radical wonder is still alive.

Questions for Further Reflection

1. In the opening dialogue the question is raised, "Why do we think in stereotypes?" How would you answer this question? Where do you think Ryan got his stereotypes? Why does he seem unwilling to question or abandon them? What characteristics of a philosopher does Sarah exhibit in this dialogue?

2. Wisdom is mentioned as an essential human virtue not only by early philosophers, but also by all the major world religions. Why has its importance seemed to diminish over the centuries? Or is this a mistaken conclusion to draw? Is it as important an excellence now as it ever was?

3. The claim is made that wonder is essential for philosophers and important for poets. Where else is it important? How is wonder different from curiosity? How is it related to reverence? What are some examples of an encounter with wonder in your own experience? How, if at all, can wonder be cultivated?

4. In the story on page 10 the physics teacher seems to believe that "because of Bernoulli's principle" actually explains something. Does it? In what sense? On page 13 the claim is made that "because of gravity" is simply a name for our ignorance. Is it? Can something be the right answer and still explain nothing? Can you think of other (perhaps clearer) examples of things that function as "names for our ignorance"?

5. This chapter characterizes philosophical questions as radical, fundamental, basic, as well as rooted in wonder. Each of these characterizations is a metaphor. How else might we characterize philosophy? How are the questions a scientist asks different from questions a philosopher might ask about science? How are the questions a historian asks different from questions a philosopher might ask about history?

6. In this chapter philosophy is defined as a function of three ideas: (1) critical reflection, (2) fundamental ideas, and (3) wonder. How does that make philosophy different from some other disciplines? Compare it explicitly to: a science discipline and a humanities discipline such as history or literary criticism. What disciplines is philosophy most like? Most unlike? Explain.

7. When have you had an experience of wonder? Was it like the experience of my colleague and his telescope or like the experience expressed in Williams's poem? How can a single experience generate responses as different as poetry, philosophy, science, and religion? Or aren't these responses as different as we usually assume?

Works Cited

Murdoch, Iris. *Metaphysics as a Guide to Morals*. London: Chatto & Windus, 1992.

———. *The Sovereignty of Good*. London: Routledge & Kegan Paul, 1970.

CHAPTER TWO

Three Common Temptations

This chapter identifies some common patterns of thinking that all of us are tempted to fall into. The dialogue illustrates one of these, and the discussion details some others and explains how they frequently handicap our thinking.

Dialogue II

Abel: Ethics is just a matter of opinion. So whatever you think is right for you is right for you. Since it's just a matter of opinion, no one can tell you you're wrong.

Baker: I don't agree, and I don't really believe you'd say that if you'd stop to think about it.

A: Why, are you some kind of moral absolutist who believes that there are authoritative moral answers written somewhere that we can know and prove to others?

B: No, I don't believe that.

A: Then you must agree with me that ethics is just a matter of opinion. Everybody's got an opinion and ethics is just a matter of opinion, so everybody's right.

B: No, I don't have to agree with you. You're making a large assumption that's messing up your thinking, namely that there are only two possibilities: (A) moral absolutism or (B) subjective relativism. Your argument works only if there aren't any other possibilities. You're arguing that it's either A or it's B; it's not A, so it must be B.

A: Well, if there are other possibilities I've never heard of them.

B: You may not have a name for them, but I think you know them all the same. Just stop and think about it a bit. Consider the work a doctor does in diagnosing an illness. Is the doctor's diagnosis an example of absolute knowledge?

A: No, at least not usually.

B: For example, doctors can sometimes disagree about their diagnoses, and sometimes make diagnoses of a hypothetical sort saying, "I might be wrong but I think this is a case of X. Let's try this medication and see what happens." That's the sort of thing they do, right?

A: Sure.

B: Well, that's an example of a kind of thinking that is neither absolute knowledge nor mere opinion. It's something in between, something I'd call reasoned belief. A case where, although we don't have absolute knowledge we don't have mere opinion either. It's a case where reasons can be given and evaluated; a case where something can be asserted and also be tested; a case where although it's possible we're wrong there are still good reasons to think we're right.

A: But how does that apply to ethics?

B: Like the doctor, we often need to figure out what is the best thing to do in a given situation. The answer may not be obvious, but that doesn't mean it's impossible either. What we hope to get are answers backed up by reasons that can be discussed and evaluated.

A: So ethical thinking is another example of reason supported belief? Is that what you're trying to say?

B: Yes. In fact I'd say that very few (if any) things qualify as absolute knowledge, and very few (if any) things are matters of mere opinion. At least all the interesting things we think about are somewhere in the middle: diagnosing illnesses, making investments, writing history, figuring out who to vote for, theorizing in science, deciding what direction your career should take, evaluating therapies in psychology, figuring out the best way to raise kids, deciding whether you should ask somebody to marry you, figuring out which car you should buy, evaluating a book. . . .

A: All right, I get the point already.

B: Sorry, I guess I got carried away with examples. But they are all issues about which reasons can be given and evaluated. In each of those cases the kinds of reasons and the methods of evaluation will be different. . . .

A: But ethics is the sort of thing about which people can be very opinionated. Doesn't that prove that it's just a matter of opinion? Some people, at least, have very strongly held opinions without having very strong reasons.

B: That's for sure. People can be opinionated about anything, about what will treat and cure diseases, for example. That's their problem, but it doesn't prove your point. Just because some people won't listen to reasons doesn't mean there aren't good reasons to be considered. Some people aren't even persuaded that the earth is round. That doesn't mean there aren't good reasons to think it is. It merely means that some people don't want to hear them or think about them.

A: OK, I see what you mean. But I'm still not so sure that ethics is just like giving diagnoses in medicine.

B: I didn't say it was just like it; certainly there are differences. I only said they are alike in the sense that they are both issues about which reasons can be given and evaluated. They both can be cases of reasoned belief.

A: Well, then, what are the reasons that you think are so relevant to ethical thinking? I'd like to hear what they are.

B: OK, I'd be happy to tell you, but I bet you already know what most of them are. I don't think these are the kinds of things you find out about by being told.

A: So you admit I do know something?

B: For sure. In fact, I'd say you know more than you give yourself credit for. In this conversation I haven't told you anything new. I've just helped you pay attention to things you already knew. The kinds of things that count as reasons in ethics are things you already know. You just need to think about it a bit.

A: OK, give me a day, then let's talk about it again.

Common Patterns of Temptation

We are all perennially tempted by many of the same things. That's why advertising works so well, because advertisers are able to predict what kinds of things will be tempting to us. If they can make us believe their product will make us look sexy, rich, or successful, we'll probably buy it because these things are a draw for most everyone. That's also why there is a perennial necessity for things like weight loss programs and self-help books. As we grow older and get to know ourselves better, we also get to know the patterns of our own temptations. I know by now, for example, how tempted I am by corn chips. If there is a bag of them around the house it is very difficult for me to leave them alone. Knowing how tempting I find them as a late night snack and how bad they are for me (being both high in fat and high in sodium), I try to avoid buying them altogether. But, I must admit, there are occasions when I fall prey to the temptation all over again.

It isn't only advertising that reveals the same patterns of human temptation. Our laws illustrate the same patterns. We have laws of the sort we have, against theft, larceny, embezzlement, murder, rape, and child abuse, because many people in all communities are tempted by much the same things. Once in a great while we need a new law to guard us against a new temptation, but most often it is simply an old temptation applied to a new situation. Here again we find ourselves falling into the same patterns of temptation over and over again.

There are temptations in thinking as well as in behavior. Here, once again, all of us are apt to fall prey to the same patterns of temptations. In fact, some of these temptations in thinking are so common to us that logicians have given them standard names, the fallacy of appeal to ignorance, the fallacy of false analogy, the fallacy of the slippery slope, and so on.

It should be instructive to us to notice that we are tempted by the same mistaken patterns of thinking over and over again. Perhaps from this we ought to learn that we aren't as original, at least in the kinds of mistakes we make, as we may have thought we were. We may see this as a cause for despair (the fact that with each generation we again are tempted to make the same mistakes) and/or as cause for celebration (the fact that we now know and are able to detect these patterns and help each other out).

This kind of learning is part of what we mean by critical thinking. A critical thinker is a person who is (1) corrigible, (i.e., open, even eager, to learning from and about his or her own mistakes), (2) aware of the kinds of mistakes people in general make in their thinking, (3) aware of the kinds of mistakes he or she, in particular, is tempted to fall prey to, and (4) attempting to embody a high standard of criticism in thinking.

As mentioned, logicians have identified a number of standard temptations in thinking and have given them standardized names. One text, S. Morris Engel's *With Good Reason: An Introduction to Informal Fallacies*, identifies over forty fallacies. For the purposes of the present discussion, however, we wish to focus on three temptations that are particularly common and troublesome to people who are beginning philosophical inquiry. We focus on them here, early in the text, because they are very influential temptations and because jointly they have shaped many of the ways we think about important issues. We hope that by identifying them early on and focusing on them as temptations for all of us, we may be able to recognize and call attention to them as they arise for us later in our discussions.

The Temptation of the Easy Answer

The Quick, Low-Effort Answer

Many of us (and most of us in at least some area of our thinking) fall prey to this temptation. A former student of mine who is now a high school math teacher tells me that her students had a three-minute tolerance for math problem solving. Any problem they couldn't figure out a way to solve in three minutes they would quit working on. She said to me, "That was one of the first things I knew I had to work on with these students. They assumed that any answer they were going to get would come easily to them. They were more handicapped by this assumption than by anything else. These intelligent students, based on this assumption, had all persuaded themselves they were math-dumb, when actually they were simply math-impatient."

This same pattern afflicts the rest of us too, sometimes in widely different areas. I have seen students make such assumptions about thinking in ethics. Somehow they have come to assume that figuring out what is the right thing to do or the best course of action to take should be an easy task. Sometimes the right thing may be obvious, but frequently it is not obvious at all. Any good parent will testify that, with the best of intentions, it is very difficult to know what is the best thing to do or the right course of action to take. Should we try to treat our children equally in spite of the fact that they have such varied abilities and needs? Should I let my son quit his team or should I encourage him to stick it out in spite of the hard time he's having with an idiotic coach? These are not questions that are easily answered, yet they are the kinds of questions that parents have to struggle with. They are difficult because they are complex, because they have so many things that impact on them, and because of the significant things at stake in answering them.

Why are we impatient with the effort that goes into thinking? Where do we get the assumption that the answer ought to be obvious and that it should require little work? Certainly laziness is part of the cause. We are all tempted occasionally to find the easy way. But I don't think that laziness by itself explains why we are tempted by the quick, low-effort answer. The same math teacher noticed the willingness of her students to put in hours of practice to improve their skills in a sport or in playing an instrument, yet assumed that math should come easily or not at all. She became convinced that their problem was not laziness, but rather *the assumption that thinking ought to be easy* even though physical skills require both much time and effort.

Where did these students get this assumption? Do we establish and reinforce this assumption in school? Unfortunately, we sometimes do. How? We reinforce the idea that answers ought to be quick and easy by teaching and testing for the answers rather than by enabling and encouraging students to make the effort of inquiry and think their way through to their own answers. We also do this by the way in which we create and use textbooks. Textbooks are frequently collections of other people's answers systematically and attractively arranged for ease of digestion. The student who learns mainly from textbooks expects that all studies will be like this (i.e., will be largely collections of information). A textbook in history, for example, might inform us of all the important events in the civil war, the places and dates on which they occurred, and so on, without ever giving us an idea about the kind of work someone had to do to discover and arrange this information. From such a textbook experience we are likely to come away thinking that history is just a collection of historical information, rather than seeing it as a disciplined process of inquiry that sorts through masses of letters, documents, and interviews in order to find out what really happened during a battle or what life was like for people living in a city on the south/north border during the Civil War. By teaching answers we create the expectation that a discipline is a set of answers rather than an inquiry requiring both time and effort to do well.

The Simple Answer

Along with the temptation toward the quick, low-effort answer comes another easy answer temptation: the temptation toward the simple answer. As H. L. Mencken (1880–1956), American newswriter and wit, once said, "For every complex question there is a perfectly simple answer—and it is wrong."

One form of simple answer we are inclined to fall for is what is often called a "half-truth." A half-truth states something that is true but only captures some fraction of the picture, particularly when the account of only a fraction of the picture can be very misleading. "Two Excedrin relieved headaches more effectively than any other brands tested in a hospital study." So ran an advertisement a few years ago. What the statement said was true, but what the statement failed to say changed the picture drastically. The same tests showed that one Excedrin was as effective as two, that a placebo was as effective as either, and that the group tested were all women who had just given birth in the last twenty-four hours. When the larger picture is known it points us toward a conclusion of a very different sort.

We encounter fractional truths frequently in political rhetoric. One campaigner may report her opponent's vote on some bill. The report may be accurate as far as it goes, but may leave out details about why the person voted as she did or what kinds of amendments or riders were attached to the bill by the time it came to a vote. Knowing such things may change our evaluation of the vote drastically, and that is, of course, why that side of the story is not told.

These are both examples of cases where others shape our perception of events by presenting the truth fractionally. But I'm sure we can also find cases where we shape our own beliefs in the same way. Sometimes we willfully do not want to hear another side of a story. Sometimes we deliberately look only for data that reinforce our own views while knowing perfectly well there are data and arguments to be heard on another side. Why do we do this? Apparently because we are happier with a single simple answer than we would be with the more complex picture that represents the reality of the case. Why should we prefer the simple, fractional answer to the more complex and fuller one? Perhaps because the simple answer reinforces some other belief or prejudice we hold, but perhaps also just because it is easier. In short, because the simple answer is more tempting. Is there something we admire in the opinionated, single point of view, "true-believer" sort of person that we do not admire in the person who sees the complexity of reality and is more hesitant to offer an opinion? Which of these two people is more likely to be a successful candidate for political office? Which one is more likely to be a frequent talk show guest? Would we really enjoy watching a careful, full-picture thinker being interviewed on TV?

Polarized, Black or White Thinking

In some ways the "easy answer" temptation embodies another temptation, the temptation to think in terms of polarized opposites, seeing everything as either black or white, all good or all bad, all true or all false. The easy answer temptation assumes the polarity, either there's an easy answer or there's no answer at all. The dialogue that opens this chapter illustrates the temptation to miss the large range of possibilities between the polarized opposites. But it also raises a question: If the range of possibilities between the polar opposites is so large (B even claims that almost nothing is at the poles and almost everything is somewhere in the middle), then why are we tempted to think in terms of polarized opposites?

I once heard someone suggest that humans are tempted by polarized thinking because we have only two hands. So we are inclined to say, "On the one hand . . . and on the other . . ." assuming those are the only possibilities we have. If only we had a third hand, or like an octopus, eight of them, we'd be more subtle thinkers, more likely to see a range of possibilities as opposed to only a few of them. Although this illustrates the problem well, I doubt whether it's the cause of our polar thinking. I think it's more likely that we fall for polar thinking because it's so simple. Putting things in one of two boxes is much easier than noticing the subtle similarities and differences in a whole range of things. So just as we saw the "easy answer" temptation as a form of the polarized thinking temptation, we may also be able to see part of the temptation of polarized thinking in the fact that it is an easy answer.

I believe another cause of our polarized thinking is that we often organize our entertainment, the stories we tell, and the learning we do around this principle. How many of our movies are basically bad guys versus good guys? How much of our political thinking embodies an "us versus them" view of things? How many of our tests are set up as true versus false? In a humanities class I was teaching we were discussing Sophocles' tragedy *Antigone*. A couple of students expressed confusion over the story because, as they said, "We don't understand who's the good guy and who's the bad guy here." Their confusion was understandable because we live in a culture in which most of the stories we tell are set up that way. The problem is that they were making an assumption that doesn't do very much justice to the subtleties and point of the story. We frequently bring the same assumption to reading narratives from the Bible. And just as frequently we find the assumption does not serve us very well. Is Saul, the first Hebrew king, a good guy or a bad guy? How about David, his successor? How about Jesus' disciple Peter?

Several years ago a colleague and I taught a course that enrolled over 200 students. We wanted to construct a final exam for the course that would be quick to grade and easy to record, so we tried to write 50 true and false questions that would test the essential material of the course. But we encountered a serious problem: things that were clearly true or false were usually extremely trivial and things that were essential and required some thought were always arguable, and consequently not simply true or false. After many hours trying to come up with good questions we abandoned our effort, concluding that the options "true/false" were not rich enough to do justice to the significant issues raised in the course. This is yet another instance where dichotomous, either/or thinking did not serve very well.

Because we know we are tempted to think in some ways that do not serve us very well, we may be more aware when we fall into these patterns. If we're more aware of them we may be better able to avoid them. If we know these are temptations for all of us, we may be able to help each other by calling them to each other's attention as we proceed. May we be willing to say, like Socrates said long ago, "About such things I am as eager to be corrected as to correct others. So, with your help, we may all be able to avoid error and find the truth."

Questions for Further Reflection

1. In Dialogue II, Baker argues (p. 18 ff.) that very few (if any) things are matters of absolute knowledge or matters of mere opinion. Is that true? Can you think of examples of things that we know absolutely (i.e., know with complete certainty and in all cases) to be true? Can you think of examples of things that are mere opinion (i.e., issues regarding which *no* reasons are relevant)?

2. At the end of Dialogue II, Baker suggests that Abel already knows what the reasons are that are relevant to thinking about ethical issues, and that he only needs to pay attention to what he already knows. What kinds of things do we learn about, if any, by being told? What kinds of things do we learn about, if any, by "paying attention to what we already know"? How should learning and teaching be organized differently in these two cases?

3. The first characteristic of a critical thinker is that he or she is a person who is corrigible. Are there people who are not corrigible, who do not want to learn of or from their own mistakes? If this happens, why is it the case? Why wouldn't everyone want to know the nature of his or her mistakes and desire to correct them?

4. Can you think of other (better) reasons than those given why we might be tempted to assume that thinking should be easy? Why do you think the math students cited adopted the "get it quick or give up" strategy? If you were their teacher, how would you help them get over it?

5. A contrast is drawn in this chapter between two approaches: (1) the opinionated, simple answer, single point of view sort of person and (2) a person who sees the complexity of reality and is therefore more hesitant to offer an opinion or assume that he or she is right. Which of these two types of people would you rather acquire as: (a) a sales-person? (b) the CEO of a corporation? (c) a judge? (d) a senator or congressperson? (e) a parent? (f) a spouse? In each case explain in detail.

6. The discussion of the temptation of polarized thinking gives three examples where such thinking does not serve us very well. Can you think of other examples where we are tempted to polarize our think-ing and consequently miss productive alternatives? Can you think of cases where polarized thinking works well?

7. How would you characterize a person who actually preferred a frac-tional view of things to seeing the full picture even after the error had been pointed out to her or him? How would you explain willful igno-rance (i.e., the ignorance of a person who is not corrigible)? Are we all guilty of this to some degree, or do most of us desire that our thinking correspond to the complexities of reality? Can you imagine someone saying, "I prefer my own illusions to the truth"?

CHAPTER THREE

Philosophy as Cultural Criticism

This chapter looks at the role of the philosopher as a social and cultural critic. How are we able to be critical of our own cultural assumptions and what happens when we do so? The chapter considers several examples of philosophical thinkers including Diogenes the Cynic, Siddhartha Gautama the Buddha, and some contemporary feminist authors. The chapter concludes by considering whether such criticism puts philosophy above culture.

Dialogue III

Carl: Today in anthropology class we talked about what it would be like to live in a small, closed, univocal culture.

Diego: What do you mean by a closed, univocal culture? These concepts are not familiar to me.

C: "Closed" means a culture that is isolated from others, where people only really know people inside their own community. "Univocal" means "one-voiced," a community where everybody thinks exactly alike.

D: You mean a place where everyone agrees about everything?

C: No, you can still have disagreements in a univocal culture, but people agree about the most basic things—for example, what reality is, how to tell truth from falsity, what characteristics of persons are to be admired and which to be condemned.

Elaine: That sounds a lot like the small town I came from. There was an awful lot of conformity to set social standards, and if you were "different" people really let you know you weren't welcome.

C: Wow! And I was about to say that I found the whole idea of a closed, univocal society to be almost unimaginable, but then you said you grew up in such a place.

D: What's so hard to imagine about it?

C: People all liking basically the same things, disliking the same things, believing the same things; they'd be like culture clones of each other. It's hard to imagine people all thinking the same way about things. The people I know disagree so fundamentally about things that they often find it hard even to communicate with each other.

D: My roommate and I are like that. At first we argued a lot, but then found out we couldn't even argue because we lacked a common ground to appeal to. It's like we were from different planets, speaking different languages. So now we just don't talk at all. I can hardly wait until the end of term so I can move out. I would much rather live in a community of like-minded people. There, at least, you have some way to settle disputes when they come up.

C: But would disputes come up at all among such people? I think they'd be pretty trivial.

E: What do you think makes a closed, univocal culture begin to change? If all the people in them are brought up in the same way, how do they ever initiate change? Where does creativity occur?

C: I suppose it happens when someone comes in from the outside, or when an insider leaves, meets people with other points of view, and then returns to the community again.

D: I think the latter is more believable. If an outsider came in, he'd just be regarded as too strange. No one would ever listen to him. I think it has to be someone who is regarded as an insider but has come to question some of the ways insiders think.

E: I remember the pastor at our church talking about this. When he graduated from the seminary, he went back to his hometown to serve his home parish. He said that was a big mistake because everybody expected him to be the same person he was when he left. They were quite offended when they discovered he had come back with some "new ideas" and different ways of doing things. He didn't stay there very long.

C: That's why I don't agree with Diego when he says that a univocal society would be better than an open, pluralistic one. I think the social pressure to think in one way would be stifling.

D: Yes, maybe so. But finding that you don't even have the ability to discuss things with others, that's horrible too. You can't even disagree significantly if you don't agree about anything. It's fun to play games like soccer or chess. But you can't play at all if you don't agree about what game you're playing. It's not even a game where one is playing soccer and the other is playing chess.

C: But it's not a game if everybody is on the same team either. Common rules are necessary, but so is some kind of opposition. You need at least two competitors to make a game, maybe also to make an interesting conversation.

E: That reminds me of an interview with some Russian artists I heard a while back on the radio. The people being interviewed were artists who, under the old, repressive Soviet regime, had been imprisoned for the political implications of their artwork. They were asked how things had changed for them in the new Russia. They said that now they could paint what they liked and exhibit where they liked and sell their paintings to U.S. art dealers and make a lot of money.

C: Sounds like an artist's paradise.

E: In a way, yes, but in some ways not at all. All of them agreed that the change hadn't been all for the good. They now had freedom to paint what they wanted—but the problem is that no one cares anymore what they do. The society is tolerant of everything and therefore bored by everything. They had gotten freedom but lost their voice along with their interested audience.

D: So a completely open society that's tolerant of everything has a hard time being interested in what's being said?

E: Yes, I guess so. What had been a significant political protest before got reduced to a mere commodity.

D: That's an implication of pluralism I hadn't thought about.

E: So what we really need is something between the two extremes. A totally closed, univocal society is stifling and static, but a totally open and pluralistic one is chaotic and banal. We need to allow for significant disagreement and freedom, yet have enough in common to make disagreement possible, yet interesting, and make freedom worth having.

D: Well said, Elaine. You know, I like this synthesis we've come up with.

C: I bet we don't come up with anything any better than this after a whole term in that anthropology class.

E: Well, let us know when the prof wants us to come in and straighten everything out.

C: Yeah, right. But don't hold your breath waiting for that to happen.

Questioning What the Culture Gives Us

Part of the experience of wonder is seeing the familiar afresh, seeing without prejudging, experiencing without putting things in all too familiar boxes. To do this the person wondering has to ask questions that aren't usually asked, puzzle about things not usually considered puzzling, and doubt things that are not usually doubted. Sometimes we must "put in brackets" what we "suppose we know" to experience fully what is given.

When I was a graduate student I made some spending money serving as a subject for experiments run in the psychology department. Among the many tests they ran on me was a series that tried to find out how thoroughly attached people are to conventional categories. In one such test the psychologist flashed a set of slide pictures very quickly on a screen and asked me to describe what I saw. At first the pictures he showed were quite normal, but after a while he would slip in some weird things, for example, a calico cat with a rhinoceros's head, or a queen of diamonds with the diamonds colored green instead of red, or an octagonal red sign that said POTS instead of STOP. In each case they wanted to see whether I would say what I "knew was right" or whether

I would say what I actually saw. At the end of the test they told me that some subjects never saw anything unusual, but saw only what they assumed was there, a kitten, a queen of diamonds, a stop sign.

In another test I was taken into a small room and told to examine the room carefully. I would be brought back there later to tell them what, if anything, had changed. I studied the objects in the room in detail, trying to notice the number and placement of chairs, pictures, lamps and so on. Before they returned me to the room they first made me put on a pair of goggles, then let me reenter. They asked me to tell them what, if anything, was different. They started the stopwatch. I looked around the room quickly taking an inventory of the furnishings: chairs, pictures, lamps and so on. Seeing nothing different I happened to glance out the window at the end of the room and suddenly noticed that the building across the street was tipping over toward us at about a 45-degree angle. I gasped, then saw that the wall at the end of the room was doing the same, and finally that all the space in the room was atilt in the same way. I told them what I saw and they pushed the button on the stopwatch. Thirty-five seconds had elapsed. At the end of the testing I asked them how my time had compared to others tested. They said only three had noticed the change immediately, and over a dozen *never* noticed the slanted space although they were left in the room with the goggles on for over an hour. This demonstrates that most people "correct" what they experience to match their assumptions about what is there, at least to some degree. I did that too as long as I was focusing on details. Only when I gave up on that project was I free to notice how the space of the room and the surrounding world had changed. The experience of wonder is like this; it is a breaking free from our assumptions of what the world is like to be able to notice anew what is actually there.

Philosophers practice this breaking through by attempting to recognize and then question the assumptions we all bring to thinking about and experiencing the world. Consequently, a large part of the discipline of philosophy is the uncovering of assumptions through the disciplined asking of questions: "Why do I value the things I do? What do I believe to be true, and on what grounds do I believe this? How does our language work? What is nonsense and what is very deep sense? Who do I take to be a model of a rational person? What is that decision based on? Our language talks about many ideas that are general and abstract, ideas like freedom, justice, space, time, the laws of nature, and human rights. Are these things real? What does 'real' mean, and what are the standards that need to be met for something to be considered such?" What these questions do is to turn our attention toward the very tools and structures we use when we think. They are *radical* questions insofar as they get at the roots of our thinking.

The Questioner and Society

What happens to people who regularly ask such questions? They become weird; that is, they experience a certain amount of cultural alienation. They question things at those points where everybody else is willing to march unquestioningly in the parade. Henry David Thoreau (1817-1862) used the following metaphor to talk about this kind of alienation:

> Why should we be in such desperate haste to succeed and in such desperate enterprises? If a man does not keep pace with his companions, perhaps it is because he hears a different drummer. Let him step to the music which he hears, however measured or far away. (Walden, p. 241)

People who question become culture critical. They may see little value in things others seem to value highly. They may see little truth in things others take as authoritative. They may see humor in others' seriousness and take very seriously what others may find trivial and tangential. The following one-liners from Diogenes the Cynic (c. 400-325 B.C.E.) express both his sense of alienation and his critical distance from things others took seriously:

> Even with a lamp in broad daylight I cannot find an honest man.

> I have come to debase the coinage.

> Stealing treasury property is particularly dangerous: big thieves are ruthless in prosecuting little thieves.

> I pissed on the leg of the man who called me a dog. Why was he surprised?

> Happy is the man who plans to marry but changes his mind, who plans a trip he does not take, who runs for public office but withdraws his name, who wants to belong to the inner circle of the influential, but is excluded.

> To a woman who had flopped down in front of an altar with her butt in the air I remarked in passing, did she not know the god was also behind her?

> Of what use is a philosopher who doesn't piss anybody off?

> I am a citizen of no city, but only of the cosmos.

Henry David Thoreau, 1817–1862

Thoreau is an original American "wonderer" if there ever was one. He made his living sometimes as a surveyor, sometimes as a school-teacher, and sometimes as a day laborer in and around his hometown of Concord, Massachusetts. But he never took any of these occupa-tions so seriously as to interrupt his sojourns in the woods of New England. He was a man of fierce independence and he frequently wrote and spoke on public issues (e.g., for the abolition of slavery), long before they became popular. In 1842 Thoreau willingly went to jail rather than pay taxes to a government that supported slavery and promoted war. This was the occasion for his writing "On the Duty of Civil Disobedience," an essay that has influenced many, including Mohandas Gandhi and Martin Luther King, Jr.

In 1845 Thoreau began an experiment in self-reliance and non-conformity, moving into a self-constructed cabin in the woods near Walden Pond. There he lived off what he could grow and harvest from nature while writing his classic, *Walden*. Included here are a few thoughts from that book.

On the vanity of work: *Men labor under a mistake. . . . By seeming fate, commonly called necessity, they are employed, as it says in an old book, laying up treasures which moth and rust will corrupt and thieves will steal. It is a fool's life(5). The mass of men lead lives of quiet despera-tion . . . and [they] work under the illusion of owning their houses. When a man has got his own house he may not be the richer but the poorer for it, and it be the house that has got him. The cost of a thing is the amount of what I will call life that must be exchanged for it (25).*

On working toward retirement: *This spending of the best part of life earning money in order to enjoy a questionable liberty during the least valuable part of it reminds me of the Englishman who went to India to make a fortune . . . in order that he might return to England and live the life of a poet (39–40). I went to the woods because I wanted to live delib-erately, to front only the essential facts of life and see if I could not learn what it had to teach, and not, when I came to die, discover that I had not lived (67).*

Unlike Diogenes, who was moved by his questioning to deflate and poke fun at his contemporaries, the philosopher may be moved with compassion to liberate people from the beliefs that limit their views of each other and the world. Such is the case in this encounter between Gautama Siddhartha (c. 563-483 B.C.E.), whom his followers referred to as "the Buddha," that is, the awakened one, and Sunita, an untouchable, (i.e., a man from the lowest caste of Hindu society), who was employed as a latrine cleaner and carrier of "nightsoil."

Sunita quickly moved off the path and made his way down to the river. When Sunita veered from the path, the Buddha did the same. Sunita was panic stricken. He hastily put the buckets of nightsoil down and looked for a place to hide. Not knowing what else to do, Sunita waded into the river and stood with his palms joined.

Curious villagers came out of their homes and lined the shore to watch what was happening. Sunita had veered off the path because he was afraid he would pollute the Buddha and his followers. He could not have guessed the Buddha would follow him. He hoped the Buddha and his followers would leave him and return to the road. But the Buddha did not leave. He walked up to Sunita and said, "Friend, come closer so that we may talk."

Sunita, his palms still joined said, "Lord, I do not dare."

"Why not?" asked the Buddha.

"I am an untouchable. I do not want to pollute you and your monks."

"On our path we no longer distinguish between castes. You are a human being like the rest of us. Only greed, hatred and delusion can pollute us. Come and become a bhikku in our community."

Sunita could not believe his ears. He said, "No one has ever spoken to me such kindness before. This is the happiest day of my life." The Buddha and his followers ordained Sunita right there and provided him with a robe.

The local people had witnessed all this take place. News rapidly spread that the Buddha had welcomed an untouchable into his community. This caused a furor among higher castes in the capital. Many condemned the Buddha for violating sacred tradition. Others suggested the Buddha was plotting to overthrow the existing order and wreak havoc in the country. (Old Path White Clondo, p. 278–281)

The philosopher may be moved to educate. Socrates did this by publicly posing the kinds of questions we listed earlier in his daily conversations with the people of his city. Socrates had said he had a kind of "divine commission" to serve as a "gadfly" to his community. His continual questioning, like the buzzing and stinging of a fly, would not let them become complacent or self-assured with things the way they were.

The philosopher may be moved to posit a source of higher knowledge than the "common opinion" based on unquestioned assumptions

---

Plato, 427–347 B.C.E.

Plato is one of those characters whose nickname has replaced his actual name, Aristocles. "Plato," in Greek, means "broad one" and it is not clear whether this nickname referred to his physique or his mind. Perhaps both.

Plato is one of only a few philosophers whose philosophical insight was matched by an extraordinary ability as a writer. Plato's dialogues are not only philosophically interesting and challenging, they are literary masterpieces. In them Plato connects a development of characters and their relationship, and an aptness of setting, with the topic under discussion. Very often he does this with a wry sense of humor and irony, showing us one thing in the dialogue while telling us something different. In *The Phaedo*, for example, Plato (in dialogue between Socrates and two Pythagorean friends) offers several arguments for the immortality of the soul, none of which stands up to criticism. At the same time he shows us the courage of Socrates, facing imminent death, yet caring more for the quality of the argument than he does for his own beliefs and comfort. In *The Republic* Socrates articulates for a group of young friends what an ideal state should look like, including in it the warning that philosophical discussions there should not include young men, but only those who have completed all the prerequisite studies including a ten-year course in mathematics. Plato does not resolve for us whether to believe what Socrates says or what Socrates does. But by creating such a tension he engages us in the philosophical enterprise in a firsthand way. The dialogue becomes alive in our midst.

---

found in the culture. Gautama Siddhartha did this by declaring that many of the things that guided the lives of most people were, upon awakening, seen to be illusions. Plato expresses this same sense of illusion and unreality of the common view with his famous analogy of people imprisoned in a cave, from his dialogue *The Republic*:

> Imagine men to be living in a cave-like dwelling, the entrance to which is far removed. The men have been there since childhood, with their necks and legs in fetters so that they remain in the same place and can only see ahead of them. Light is provided by a fire burning behind them. Between the fire and the prisoners is a path across the cave and along this a low wall, like the screen at a puppet show. Men carry along that wall so as to show above

it, all sorts of artefacts, cut-outs of men and animals so that their shadows project against the wall of the cave. If these shadows were all they had ever seen don't you suppose these prisoners would take these shadows to be real things?

Suppose one of them was freed and had to stand up and walk toward the light. Doing this would give him pain, would it not? Suppose he was shown the cut-outs that had produced the shadows he had seen before, then the fire itself, and finally forced up toward the entrance into the daylight. Would he not be inclined to turn around and rush back into the cave where he was familiar? But eventually he might be able to perceive the realities that he had previously seen the cut-outs of, and before that the shadows of the cut-outs. Then, at last, he might be able to see the sun, and contemplate how it is this light that provides the seasons and the sustenance for everything else there is.

When he then reflects on his previous condition would he not consider himself happy to have made the change and consider those who remained imprisoned in the cave with pity? If this man were forced to return to the cave and compete with the other prisoners in seeing the shadows—would he not be ridiculed or considered blind? Would he not be evidence to those imprisoned that one must never make such an upward journey?

This whole image must be related to what we said previously. The world of the cave is our life in the visible world. The journey upward toward the light is the journey of the soul to the intelligible realm, compared to which the visible realm is a mere shadow-reality. The Good itself is the last to be known, and like the sun in our story it illumines and sustains everything else. Education, then, is this process of turning around and moving from darkness to light, from unreality toward our knowledge of the most real. (514a–517)

How does society respond to philosophers? Usually in a double-minded way, just as religious communities have responded to prophets. The people of ancient Jerusalem, at one point willing to put the prophet Jeremiah to death, later regard his message as the word of the Lord and preserved it as part of their sacred scriptures. So the initial reaction to philosophical questioning is frequently a negative one: Diogenes was honored by only a few in his own day. Most people treated him as they thought he lived, "like a dog," hence the name they called him that he later adopted for himself, namely "Cynic," which means "dog" in Greek. Siddhartha had many followers who formed a community around him, but most people, like the crowd in the story, probably regarded him as an impious troublemaker. Socrates was tried, convicted, and sentenced to death for "impiety and corrupting the youth." Later, of course, people came to find the lives and teachings of such people to be extremely valuable. Jeremiah's words, despised while he lived, became part of sacred scripture later on. We now think about the Athenian citizens not because of their own importance or authority, but because they were the prosecutors of Socrates. We read about the citizens of the village in northern India because of their righteous anger at Siddhartha, and we are now interested in the Concord village jailhouse only because it once held Thoreau. These individuals, all willing to critique elements of their culture, have now become their culture's best known representatives.

The Need for Social Criticism

Does society need criticism? Yes, I have never heard of one that did not. Every society embodies a lot of assumptions that reinforce ideas of who has authority, power and prestige, who is in and who is out, who is righteous and who is impious, who is simple and who is sophisticated. In order to be thought well of by our fellows we buy into this pattern of thinking, and having made an investment in it, we find it very difficult to question. Like the royal retinue and the citizens in the children's story, "The Emperor's New Clothes," we go along with a lot of nonsense simply because we fear the derision of others if we question it. Individuals willing to question such things, like the young child in that story, actually do the rest of us a big favor. We may not perceive it as such, but without their liberating questioning the rest of us are often trapped, like Sunita, fearfully living out the consequences of our culture's way of doing things.

Any society that values creativity also needs to enable criticism. If we cannot question the way we are doing things and thinking about things at present, it will not occur to us that they could be thought of or done differently. Siddhartha's noble experiment, a society where caste did not count for anything, was not possible without a willingness to question something that "everybody" accepted as a fact, namely that people belonged in social castes. Socrates' embodiment of a mode of education based on critical dialogue is possible only where someone has dared to question the assumptions surrounding the ideas of knowledge, authority, and learning dominant in the society. It only occurs to us to try to create better laws if we see the imperfections in our present ones. So philosophy is important partly because cultural criticism is so important.

Two Temptations

But there is a danger here as well, one that is a particular temptation for philosophers. If most of us live in the darkness of the cave, or live under the dominance of illusion, shouldn't we give authority to those who have seen the light and have been awakened? Many people would say yes. That is why they follow the teachings of those they believe to be so enlightened. That is why some philosophers have disciples. The danger, of course, is that the philosopher, or her teachings, will become the new "unquestionable authority," and a new system of ideas that must not be questioned will have replaced the old one.

Fortunately many of the best thinkers have seen this problem in advance and have tried to address it. In Buddhism, for example, one is meant to follow the teachings of Siddhartha, but one is also advised that in the process of pursuing the Buddha, "if you find the Buddha, kill him." Socrates, on the day of his death, noticed that those who revered him were treating him as already dead by being unwilling to question fiercely what he had said. So he admonishes them to care more about the truth and the life of the argument than they care about him. Philosophy must, in other words, bring the same fierceness to self-criticism as it brings to the criticism of the culture. The analogy of the cave needs in turn to be questioned because it always runs the risk of setting up a new hierarchy of truth and falsehood, higher and lower, insiders and outsiders, righteous and sinners.

The other temptation involved in culture criticism is the assumption that one can transcend the problems of culture-embedded thinking. If every culture can be criticized, one might think, why not shed all one's cultural assumptions completely and conduct one's thinking from some point of view that transcends culture? If all cultures make unwarranted assumptions, why not do philosophy in a way that is acultural or supracultural and avoids making any assumptions altogether? That this is a seductive philosophical temptation is witnessed to by the number of good philosophers who have tried it.

René Descartes (1596–1653), for example, wrote that on completing his education at "one of the most celebrated schools in all Europe," and finishing "the course of studies which usually admits one to the ranks of the learned," he felt as if he knew nothing. Although he had learned the classics his culture valued, they were to him, "very superb and magnificent palaces built only on mud and sand." Thus he set out to doubt everything he had learned and to readmit into his mind only those things that were so clear and certain as to be completely beyond doubt. What an admirable ambition, to replace all the doubtful things one's culture would have one believe with things that had passed the test of being beyond doubt! What Descartes did not realize is that, although he believed he had rid himself of unwarranted assumptions, he had brought some with him, chief among them being his set of criteria for what is indubitable. His model for indubitability was mathematics; consequently he set out to establish a method that would put philosophical inquiry on a par with mathematical reasoning. This caused him to dismiss as false some things he clearly shouldn't have, and to accept as true some things he should have questioned more severely.

Benedict Spinoza (1632–1677) similarly sought a knowledge of the nature of things untarnished by common opinion. So he set out to describe the nature of things, not from the point of view of the sixteenth century renegade Jewish thinker he was, but, as he put it, *sub specie aeternitatis*, that is, from the point of view of eternity. But once again we have a philosopher who did not recognize how much cultural luggage he carried with him. Embodied in his language, and consequently in the concepts and categories he used when he thought, were a whole bundle of assumptions about substance, space, time, the nature of knowledge, and rationality. Even though Spinoza succeeded in freeing himself from some of the patterns of thinking of his contemporaries, he did not succeed in becoming culture free. His work, like the work of all thinkers, is limited in some way by the cultural and historical framework in which he thought.

The work of both Descartes and Spinoza should be read by anyone who is serious about the pursuit of philosophy. Here they are cited only as examples of thinkers who made a mistake, but they should also be read as examples of thinkers who were profound questioners and influential theorists.

It is not only earlier thinkers who fall prey to this temptation. We can find many of the same sort in our own century. There are philosophers who have claimed, not so much to have transcended culture, but to have burrowed beneath it, describing not the culture-interpreted world, but the realm of "things in themselves." Or philosophers have claimed to find the fundamental facts of the world described in primitive "atomic sentences" out of which all thought was assumed to be built.

The Culture Locatedness of Philosophy

It's dangerous to say in advance that something simply cannot be done, but it is fairly safe to say every philosopher who has tried to assume an acultural or subcultural or culture-transcendent viewpoint has failed. What should we conclude from the history of philosophy about this?

1. Although the thought of a given person may differ from that of her culture in many ways, it is also inevitably shaped by some part of that culture.

2. We may be free enough from the confines of our cultural pattern to critique it and to think of creative alternatives to it, but we are never completely free from it.

3. The best kind of objectivity we can achieve, therefore, is not to attempt being acultural, a citizen "only of the cosmos" as Diogenes claimed. Instead, we should realize what our working assumptions are and where they have come from, the ways they serve us and the ways they handicap us.

4. Our culture awareness must also be matched by our self-awareness and our culture criticism by our readiness to be self-critical.

5. Our philosophical thinking should always be done in humility, realizing it is always a thought in process. We should realize our philosophical conclusions are hypothetical (i.e., true only if certain things are assumed). We must reveal as fully as we can what is contained in the "if clause" of our thinking.

6. Our philosophical pronouncements should be made with a degree of irony, realizing that finality is a temptation and not a reality.

If all of our thinking has a cultural location, what is the nature of this cultural viewpoint in which we find ourselves? Many philosophers have pointed out that it consists of our language, the concepts in which we think, and the categories with which we perceive the world. Some philosophers, like Karl Marx, believe our thinking is also shaped by our economic class. More recently some philosophers have argued that our thinking is shaped by our gender and that women, by the very fact that they are women, think and perceive the world differently than males in the same culture. Thus it has been one of the projects of recent feminist thought to identify both the biases built into male thought patterns and to articulate the female worldview and give it a legitimate voice in philosophical discourse. The titles of several recent books by feminist authors suggest such a project: Carol Gilligan's *In A Different Voice: Psychological Theory and Women's Development*; Jane Duran's *Toward a Feminist Epistemology*; Susan Hekman's *Gender and Knowledge: Elements of a Postmodern Feminism*; *Philosophy in a Feminist Voice: Critiques and Reconstructions,* edited by Janet A. Kourany; and *Women's Ways of Knowing: The Development of Self, Voice and Mind* by Belenky, Clinchy, Goldberger, and Tarule.

Questions for Further Reflection

1. Dialogue III contrasts a closed, univocal culture to an open, pluralistic one. In what ways is American society like each of these? Where are we most tolerant of questioning? At what level? Where least tolerant? Where are we most likely to be pluralistic? Where most univocal?

2. Several examples are offered of situations where people experience what they "know is right" rather than what is actually there. Can you give other examples of this phenomenon, where our assumptions shape our thinking and even our experience? What could a person do to try to avoid this?

3. A certain amount of cultural alienation occurs with people who question their own culture's assumptions. Can you think of contemporary examples of such alienation? Who are the most radical questioners in our society? What are the symptoms of their alienation? Are there other ways that people become alienated than through philosophical questioning?

4. The story about Sunita and the Buddha illustrates the consequences of challenging well-established ways of thinking about things. How do you suppose the shocked citizens reacted to what Siddhartha was doing? How would he have responded? Are there well-established "castes" that we use for categorizing people today? Who, if anyone, is challenging them?

5. Plato's analogy of the cave dwellers contrasts those who live in illusion and darkness with those who have been enlightened. This is a metaphor we find in many places, philosophies and religions included. What are the benefits and dangers of using such a metaphor? In what way is this metaphor a particular temptation for philosophers?

6. This chapter suggests that Socrates is still the best model for philosophers. Following such a model, what should cultural criticism look like? How might following Socrates' example have helped Descartes and Spinoza avoid the difficulties they got into? Who do you think is the best example of a responsible cultural critic?

7. Do you think that gender shapes the way we think about and experience the world? If so, what are some examples? If not, why not? Does it make sense not only to talk about differences between Western and Eastern approaches to science but also differences between male approaches and female ones? Or is science, when properly done, always the same no matter who we are or where we come from?

Works Cited

Thoreau, Henry David. *Walden*. New York: Harper & Row, 1958.

The myth of the cave is freely edited and adapted from Plato, *The Republic*, translated by W.A.Grube. Indianapolis and Cambridge: Hackett Publishing, 1974.

The sayings of Diogenes the Cynic can be found in *Herakleitos and Diogenes*, translated by Guy Davenport. San Francisco: Grey Fox Press, 1979.

The version of the Buddha/Sunita story included in this chapter comes from Thich Nhat Hanh, *Old Path White Clouds: Walking in the Footsteps of the Buddha*. Berkeley: Parallax Press, 1991.

Belenky, Mary Field, Blythe McVicker Clinchy, Nancy Rule Goldberger, and Jill Matuck Tarule. *Women's Ways of Knowing: The Development of Self, Voice and Mind*. New York: Basic Books, 1986.

Duran, Jane. *Toward a Feminist Epistemology*. Savage, MD: Rowman & Littlefield, 1991.

Gilligan, Carol. *In A Different Voice: Psychological Theory and Women's Development*. Cambridge: Harvard University Press, 1982.

Hekman, Susan J. *Gender and Knowledge: Elements of a Postmodern Feminism*. Boston: Northeastern University Press, 1983.

Kourany, Janet A., ed. *Philosophy in a Feminist Voice: Critiques and Reconstructions*. Princeton: Princeton University Press, 1998.

CHAPTER FOUR

Philosophy as Cultural Conservation

Chapter Three focused on the philosopher as social and cultural critic. This chapter focuses on another side of philosophy—its more conservative aspect—as supporter and defender of cultural values. The dialogue considers whether it is possible to only be critical without declaring any beliefs of one's own. The discussion presents three examples of contemporary thinkers who combine the critical and conservative dimensions of philosophy in their work: Suzi Gablik, Ivan Illich, and Roger Scruton.

Dialogue IV

Dory: I'm very curious about you, Craig. What exactly do you believe in?

Craig: I'm not sure I believe in anything. At least I can't tell you, "This I believe."

D: I find *that* hard to believe. Everybody believes in something.

C: I don't.

D: Why? I don't understand why you wouldn't want to believe in something. I, for example, believe in equality of opportunity, I believe that my parents love me and care about me, I believe that people aren't completely happy until they are loved and have found someone they can love. I . . .

C: Hey, if you don't believe anything then you can never be proved wrong. You can never be disillusioned if you don't have any illusions.

D: But you talk as if being proved wrong is the worst thing. I think having nothing to believe in is worse than being proved wrong.

C: But believing something just because it's good to do so makes us gullible, doesn't it? I don't want to be gullible.

D: I don't know what the opposite of gullible is; maybe there isn't any single word for it. Let's call it belief-o-phobia. I think that's worse.

C: I don't agree.

D: Then you do believe something—that gullibility is worse than belief-o-phobia!

C: That's not fair! That's a belief you invented, not one I actually had.

D: What do you mean, it's a belief I invented? You said you didn't think it was worse, so that makes it your belief, doesn't it?

C: I can't have a belief without knowing that I have it, and that's not a belief I knew I had.

D: But certainly we can discover that we believe things we didn't know we believed. The beliefs we have aren't listed somewhere in our brains like the movies on the marquee at an eight-screen movie theater. So I don't see why it isn't possible to discover we have beliefs we didn't know we had. Haven't you ever read a book or an essay and said to yourself, "Though I've never thought about this topic before, what this author says is absolutely right?"

C: Yeah, I guess I've had that experience. But there's still something odd about saying that I have beliefs that I don't know I have. If I don't want to have any beliefs I don't have to have any.

D: C'mon, you have all sorts of beliefs: about who you are, about your past history, about who your family is, about what stuff is yours. I bet if someone stole your car you'd be really upset, and if you didn't have any beliefs at all I don't see how anything like that could upset you. A person who cares about something has to have some beliefs.

C: But why is it that if you ask me what they are I can't think of a single one? I think that proves I don't have any.

D: No, that only proves you're not reflective or, worse, that you'll say anything to prevail in an argument. You're impossible as well as unbelievable!

C: Maybe, but I'm still unbelieving. Don't forget that.

Criticism and Conviction

In reading Chapter Three you may have concluded that philosophers are conceptual rebels, trying to undermine or overthrow the more or less univocal cultures in which they find themselves. This rebellious image of the philosopher may fit some rather well. Diogenes blatantly announced, for example, that he had "come to debase the coinage." Friedrich Nietzsche is another example that comes to mind. In his writings he announced his intention to "transvalue all values" and wrote in a way designed to offend almost everyone. At one time or another in his writing Nietzsche attacked Christianity, Judaism, Buddhism, Jesus, Socrates, Plato, contemporary science, Germans, Italians, the English, the French, Europeans in general, women, historians, and, not the least, philosophers.

But even in such extreme cases the philosophers argue against much of what they find in society in order to point in the direction of something of genuine value that they believe the society has forgotten or diminished. In every case I know of, philosophers *argue against* some things while *arguing for* something else, and this something else is almost never a brand-new idea, but an old value that has somehow been lost or fallen out of sight. Philosophers are the challengers of some cultural values, and they are often the conservators of others.

Socrates is once again an interesting case to recall. He is brought to trial by some of his fellow Athenians on two general charges: impiety and being a corrupting influence on the youth of Athens. In the account of the trial, related in Plato's *Apology*, we hear some of the specific charges—that Socrates refuses to believe in the traditional divinities and that he has invented new divinities of his own. Yet in Socrates' defense we discover that Socrates takes his religious obligations very seriously, in fact that he sees his entire philosophical mission as one he has a divine "calling" to pursue. He says,

> [T]he story I tell does not originate with me. . . . I call upon the god at Delphi [i.e., Apollo] as witness to the existence and nature of my wisdom, if I have any at all. You remember Chairephon. . . . He went to Delphi at one time and dared to ask the oracle . . . whether any man was wiser than I, and the Pythian replied that no one was wiser. Chairephon is dead, but his brother here will testify to the truth of this. When I heard this I asked myself, "Whatever can the god mean?" . . . I am very aware that I am not wise at all ... but surely the god does not lie. (20e–21a)

So Socrates explains how it was that he was led to question all those of his contemporaries who were reputed to be wise. But in the process of questioning he found none of them lived up to their reputations. Many of those he questioned became indignant at thus being shown up as lacking the wisdom they had claimed for themselves.

> What is probable, gentlemen, is that, in fact, it is the god alone who is wise and his oracle meant that human wisdom is worth little . . . saying: "The man among you is wisest who, like Socrates, understands his wisdom is worthless. . . . So even now I continue on as the god commissioned me—I go about seeking out anyone, citizen or stranger, whom I suppose to be wise. . . . Because of this occupation, I do not engage in politics to any extent, nor do I take care of my own fortunes, for, as everyone knows, I live in great poverty because of this service to the god. (23b)

Far from being impious, a destroyer of ideals, and a corrupter of the young, we find that Socrates is very pious, takes ideals extremely seriously, much more so than his contemporaries, for he is willing to die for his beliefs. In the dialogue named after him, Socrates' friend, Crito, tries to convince Socrates to escape from prison.

> Crito: Many people, Socrates, will suppose that I could have saved you if I were willing to spend the money, but that I was too stingy to do so. Surely there can be no worse reputation than that a man is thought to value wealth more highly than he values his friends. . . .
>
> Socrates: [W]e must examine whether we should act as you suggest or not . . . I am the sort of man who pursues only that course of action which, on reflection, seems best to me. I cannot, now that this misfortune is upon me, act otherwise. . . . The only valid

consideration . . . is whether we will be acting justly. . . . If this course of action is unjust, then we have no need to take other things into account. . . . for it is clearly better to suffer and to die than to be guilty of doing wrong. (44c–48d)

So in Socrates we have a philosopher who, because of his questioning, appeared not to take the values of his culture seriously. But in actuality he was a fierce defender and conserver of them. Socrates, who appeared to be a challenger and, to some, a destroyer of values, turns out to be one of the most conservative of men. From this example we should learn to use terms like *radical* and *conservative* with care. A person who appears radical may, in another way, be extremely conservative. And the reverse may also be true.

Three Contemporary Thinkers

In the remainder of this chapter we look briefly at the work of three contemporary thinkers, Suzi Gablik, Ivan Illich, and Roger Scruton, as examples of the way a person who is critical of the culture may also argue to protect and conserve some parts of it. I have included the ideas of these particular thinkers because (1) Their ideas and arguments are accessible (i.e., they are fairly easy to understand even by readers with limited backgrounds). (2) Their views are summarizable without, I hope, unnecessarily oversimplifying them. If you find fault with the incompleteness of their arguments, please blame that on the brevity of my summaries rather than assuming a deficiency in their arguments. (3) Their views illustrate the variety of approaches philosophical thinking may take and the wide range of subjects that thinkers find interesting. (4) Their ideas and arguments are provocative, inviting further reflection on these issues. I hope that being introduced to their ideas here will make you want to read their work in its entirety.

Suzi Gablik: The Social Reconnection of Art

Suzi Gablik (1934–present) is an unusual combination of practicing artist, critic, and theoretician about the arts. She is known for championing many artists whose work is outside the mainstream of the art world including a New York group of women artists that calls itself "The Guerrilla Girls." She is the author of several books including *Has Modernism Failed?* (1991), *Conversations Before the End of Time* (1995), and *The Reenchantment of Art* (1997), discussed briefly in what follows. In that work Gablik writes:

> The prevailing attitude of mind of a culture, its world view or mind-set, is commonly called a paradigm. . . . [I]t influences the way we think, how problems are solved, what goals we pursue and what we value. The socially dominant paradigm is seldom, if ever, stated explicitly, but it unconsciously defines reality for most people. . . . [I]f our model of culture is faulty or disordered, then we ourselves are disordered in precisely the same way. (2–3)

Gablik argues that this cultural paradigm is partly established and maintained by the ways we think about and institutionalize the arts in our society. Modernist culture and its accompanying view of art has stressed the complete autonomy of art ("art for art's sake") aimed at preserving the social irrelevance and "purity" of the arts. The arts, according to this modernist view, belong in museums and other institutions like them, not embedded in the everyday life of the community. This autonomy was accompanied by a romantic, rebellious "hero" image of the artist; alienated from and not well understood by the public. As examples of such a modernist view, she quotes the critic Cyril Connoly: "From now on an artist will be judged only by . . . his solitude and the quality of his despair." And Adolph Gottlieb: "I'd like more status [as an artist] than I have now but not at the cost of closing the gap between artist and public." And finally Georg Baselitz: "The artist is not responsible to anyone. His social role is asocial . . . there is no communication with any public whatsoever." An example of a modernist work might be Marcel Duchamp's *Fountain*. It consisted of a common porcelain urinal mounted upside down on the wall of a gallery and signed by the artist, "R. Mutt." Art, in this view, is excellent when it is object focused, difficult, remote, inaccessible, and socially disturbing. Gablik also refers to it as "hyper-masculinized."

In contrast to this modernist view of art and artist, Gablik sketches a view she considers postmodern. She tries deliberately to connect art and the artist with the public, to communicate, to collaborate, to be person focused, and to be socially and environmentally responsible. Consider just two of the examples of artists whose work Gablik describes approvingly in her book.

Mierle Laderman Ukeles, a performance artist, reconstructed two locker rooms used by New York sanitation workers side by side in a New York gallery. One was furnished with what the sanitation workers called "mungo," objects retrieved from garbage. The other was a new facility: clean, shiny, outfitted with computers and exercise equipment for the personal use of the sanitation workers. The large glass facade of the gallery was written over, graffiti style, with the derogatory names that sanitation workers are frequently called while on the job. Each of the visitors to the show, including the mayor and several city council members, were handed a bucket and sponge as they entered and asked to help wash away the names and clean the windows. This work was called *Cleansing the Bad Names.*

Sculptor Bradley McCallum created a nonprofit organization called Collaborative Urban Sculpture. McCallum had noticed how reliant homeless people are on discarded shopping carts and on packing boxes and bus-waiting benches. They store and carry all their worldly possessions in the former and often sleep on, in, or under the latter. McCallum began the project of building combination shopping carts and portable shelters for these street people, custom designing them to meet the needs of those who would be using them. The constructions McCallum thought of as *useful* urban sculptures, designed and built with the collaboration and consent of its users.

These two examples do not easily fit the dominant culture's view of art. Art is not usually meant to initiate social awareness or change, nor is art usually designed to be useful. It is most often made as a commodity to be sold or an object to be located in a museum where it may not even be touched, much less be *used* by anyone.

Gablik's argument implies not only a changed view of art and its place in our society, but also a changed view of the self of the artist and the model of creativity operative in it. Modernist art emphasizes the lone, "separatist" self, Gablik asserts. Postmodern art like the examples here, in contrast, emphasizes a connected and essentially communicative self. The artist in the former case creates by challenging society with something shockingly new. The artist in the second case creates by an act of social or cultural healing.

Ivan Illich: Disestablishing School

Ivan Illich (1926–present), Austrian born, lived and worked for many years in Cuernavaca, Mexico. He now teaches at the University of Pennsylvania. He is well known as a defender of the rights and the pride and self-sufficiency of the world's poor. Illich is a critic of many modern institutions, which, although they promise to help the poor, actually exacerbate their poverty. Besides *De-Schooling Society*, discussed here, he is the author of *Shadow Work* (1981), a critique of consumerist economics; *Medical Nemesis* (1982), a critique of the health professions; and *Disabling Professions* (1987), a critique of social and psychological professionals.

Illich argues for the disestablishment of school. He does not suggest that schools should be eliminated. Instead "disestablishment" means that we should no longer make schooling compulsory, nor should we obligate people to complete a particular curriculum nor require a certain number of years of schooling to be certified for any line of work. Instead of focusing on schooling, Illich argues, we should focus on learning. Instead of focusing on school-related certification, we should focus on performance and knowledge assessment, letting the person demonstrate what she knows and is able to do, no matter where or by what means such skill or knowledge was gained.

School, Illich maintains, is but one example of the way we confuse process and substance, or confuse institutions with the values they are supposed to serve. Illich states,

> Medical treatment is mistaken for health care, social work for the improvement of community life, police protection for safety, military poise for national security, the rat race for productive work. Health, learning, dignity, independence, and creative endeavor are defined as little more than the performance of the institutions which claim to serve these ends. (1)

Most of these institutions, Illich argues, do not serve these ends very well but expend vast energy justifying and maintaining themselves. Does the legal profession, for example, serve well the end of equal justice for all? Illich believes it serves the end of creating a need for its own services, creating excess litigation and legal hurdles over which ordinary people have to leap.

School, Illich argues, does much the same thing. It persuades us that learning and taking courses are the same thing and that lack of schooling is equal to stupidity. Illich writes,

> Half of the people in the world never set foot in a school . . . yet they have learned quite effectively the message which school teaches: that they should have school, and more and more of it. School instructs them in their own inferiority. . . . So the poor are robbed of their self-respect by subscribing to a creed that grants them salvation only through the school. (42)

Illich maintains that disestablishing school would make several common practices illegal. It should be as illegal to establish school as it now is to establish a particular religion. Just as we may not now use race or creed as criteria for hiring, so we ought to make inquiries about schooling illegal in hiring, voting, or admission to public institutions. This would not exclude testing for relevant competencies, but it would exclude requiring a certain number of schooling units as a requirement for a job. "To detach competence from curriculum," Illich states, "inquiries into a man's schooling history must be made taboo, like inquiries into his political affiliation, church attendance, lineage, sexual preferences or racial background" (17).

What does Illich propose should replace schooling as a means to education? Illich does not propose one thing, but suggests a number of possibilities that individuals be left free to choose among: (1) learning skills and a trade in the old-fashioned way—through apprenticeship with a master practitioner; (2) networking with others who desire to learn similar things; (3) using learning centers that, like public libraries, would become repositories of learning resources; (4) advertising in an educational "Personals Column" for a teacher of Russian, a tutor in calculus, a study partner for a civil service exam, or an apprenticeship in snowshoe making for example. Illich concludes,

> A good educational system should have three purposes: it should provide all who want to learn with access to available resources at any time in their lives; empower all who want to share what they know to find those who want to learn it from them; and finally, furnish all who want to present an issue to the public with the opportunity to make their challenge known. (108)

Roger Scruton: Philosophy as Conceptual Ecology

Roger Scruton (1944–present), British born and educated, presently teaches at the University of London. In addition to *An Intelligent Person's Guide to Philosophy* (1998), discussed here, he is the author of *Art and Imagination: A Study in the Philosophy of Mind* (1974), *A Short History of Modern Philosophy* (1981), and *The Xanthippic Dialogues* (1993). Scruton is also a music critic whose reviews are frequently published in both England and the United States and broadcast on the BBC.

Scruton begins by contrasting the task of philosophy in the present age with the task of philosophy as it's traditionally understood. He writes,

> Philosophy in our tradition has assumed the existence of a plain, commonsense approach to things which is the property of ordinary people and which it is the business of philosophy to question. (14)

In the present day, however,

[T]here are no certainties, and no common culture worth the name. Doubt is the refrain of popular communication, skepticism extends in all directions, [so] philosophy has been deprived of its traditional starting point in the faith of a stable community.

Unlike the great Athenians we live in a crowded world of strangers, from which standards of taste have all but disappeared, in which the educated class retains no common culture, and in which knowledge has been parceled out into specialisms, each asserting its own monopoly. (11-12)

What, then, is the role of philosophy in such a polyvocal and deconstructed world? Scruton's argument is that philosophy must become self-consciously conservative, just as environmentalism is conservative. Its role is "to thoughtfully restore what has been thoughtlessly damaged" (15). Scruton asserts, "Philosophy is important, therefore, as an exercise in conceptual ecology" (25).

What ideas, specifically, is it philosophy's task to restore? Scruton examines several—including discussions of sex, music, and God—but we focus on only two here: (1) A recovery of the different senses of the question "Why?" including the sense that seeks not a causal explanation but quests after *meaning*. (2) A vindication of the holistic meaning of moral *personhood*.

1. Science seeks and offers us causal explanations. But we are often seduced by the success of science into believing this is the only legitimate way to ask and answer the question "Why?" Yet there are many things that a causal explanation does not address at all. If a judge asks me, "Why did you put arsenic in your wife's tea?" I cannot answer, "Because electrical impulses from my brain caused my hand to tip it into the teacup." Although this account may be true, it is quite irrelevant because it misconstrues the question which asks for a reason, not a cause. "The question 'Why?' when asked of a smile, is seeking a meaning," Scruton states. And the answer we seek in such a case, "makes the smile intelligible. The why of a note in music, or a line in painting is like this" (23).

The problem occurs not in the doing of science but when we suppose that conceptions that have no place in scientific explanations therefore have no reality in the world. When we describe human actions without understanding them as patterns of meanings, when we see a smile merely as a neural response, when we look at sex apart from ideas of love and belonging, as mere organ functions, we have "disenchanted" the ordinary human world, and made it, perhaps in spite of ourselves, less hospitable to human life in all its dimensions.

2. The idea of personhood depends on a form of life that is itself connected to a way of using language. Language allows for the possibil-

ity of new dimensions of social relationship. It allows, Scruton maintains, for the possibility of asking for, giving, and evaluating reasons, critiquing one's own and others' conduct, giving and asking consent, changing someone's mind by persuasion, negotiation, stating and accepting obligations, recognizing someone's sovereignty over their own body and life, and so on. Through such discourse the moral person is created and exists. Apart from the possibility of such ways of communicating the moral self is eroded. "The concept of the person exists," Scruton explains, "because we relate to each other as individuals and because the individuality of the self and other is sacred in our dealings" (69).

Philosophy is important to us in the current age, Scruton states,

> precisely because it, and it alone, can vindicate the concepts
> through which we understand and act on the world: concepts like
> that of the person, which have no place in science but which
> describe what we understand when we relate to the world as it
> truly is for us. (24)

Questions for Further Reflection

1. Is it even conceivable that a philosopher could be critical of everything without ever arguing for anything? Do you know anyone who is like this? Is it a tempting position to occupy? Why or why not? Is Craig a believable character in the dialogue? Is he correct in thinking he believes nothing or is he asserting this, as Dory suggests, merely to be stubborn and to prevail in the argument?

2. Can you think of other examples of works of art that fit the modernist paradigm? Can you think of examples that fit Gablik's postmodern model? What are your reactions to Duchamp's Fountain? To the Ukeles and McCallum projects? Can you think of reasons why these should not be considered genuine works of art? What criteria ought to determine that?

3. Gablik briefly refers to the modernist paradigm as "hypermasculinized." Is there something about the modernist view that justifies calling it masculine? Would you call Gablik's view feminist? Why or why not?

4. Is Illich correct in his analysis of the ways in which we confuse process for substance and institutions for the values they're meant to serve? Are the health professions, social work, the police, the legal system, and the school all good examples of such confusion? What do you think is a good example of an institution that serves well its intended ends?

5. Does school enable and empower learning? If school does not do this very well then why are we willing to invest so much money and time in it? What do you think of Illich's alternatives to established schooling? How do you think the "educational Personals Column" would work? Does anything like that exist now? Are there some areas of learning where we almost always ask persons to demonstrate their knowledge or abilities and almost never ask to see a diploma, a certificate, or its equivalent?

6. Suppose, as Scruton suggests, that the role of philosophy is "to thoughtfully restore what has been thoughtlessly damaged." What kinds of things, besides those mentioned, should philosophy be at work restoring? What are the damaging forces in these cases? What form should such "conceptual ecology" take?

7. Scruton allows that it is the job of science to ask "the why of causality." Is that all science does? What enterprises ask the why that seeks a reason or a meaning? Are these, reason and meaning, the same thing or are they answers to different ways of asking why? Which of these senses of the question does philosophy ask when it asks why?

Works Cited

Gablik, Suzi. *The Reenchantment of Art*. New York and London: Thames & Hudson, 1991.

Illich, Ivan. *Deschooling Society*. New York: Harper & Row, 1970.

Scruton, Roger. *An Intelligent Person's Guide to Philosophy*. New York and London: Allen Lane–The Penguin Press, 1998.

Passages from Plato's *Apology* and *Crito* are adapted from *The Trial and Death of Socrates*, translated by G.M.A. Grube. Indianapolis and Cambridge: Hackett, 1975.

CHAPTER FIVE

Philosophy and the Labyrinth of Language

This chapter focuses on the way language shapes thought. The dialogue demonstrates this by the way a question determines an agenda of possible answers and may limit the way we think about things. The discussion argues that philosophy must become aware of the agendas embodied in the language and be able to question them. Four examples are considered: (1) some advantages of process-focused language over thing-focused language; (2) Lewis Carroll's grammatical twisting of languages in his Alice *stories; (3) René Descartes's account of the relation of the concepts mind and body; (4) Robert Coles's account of how psychiatrists categorize patients but may break through to questioning their categories and their therapeutic efficacy.*

Dialogue V

Ellen: I've told you about my religious beliefs, Fred, so please tell me about yours.

Fred: That would be very hard for me to do.

E: Why? Some things we believe, some we don't believe, and some we're still uncertain about. Just arrange things that way. Start by telling me what you believe. For example, do you believe there is a God or not? You've got three answers available to you: yes, no, and uncertain.

F: What if none of those choices fit my situation very well?

E: Why wouldn't they? Which one comes closest to expressing your belief?

F: I suppose if I really had to choose among one of the three, I'd choose the "uncertain" option, over and over again, but even that doesn't exactly fit right.

E: Why not?

F: Saying that I'm uncertain (located as a choice alongside yes and no) makes it sound like if I simply had more evidence or more information I'd be able to answer with a definite "yes" or "no." But that isn't my problem.

E: Are you one of those people who finds it hard to believe in things they can't observe directly? We believe in electrons and other sub-atomic particles, yet not because anybody has directly observed them. So—

F: No, that's not the problem. But the example of electrons may be helpful because I'd have the same problem answering your question if it had been about electrons.

E: Why, if not because they can't be observed?

F: I'm not skeptical about whether electrons exist, I'm skeptical about whether "electron" and the other language we use to describe sub-atomic "particles" is the right way to describe the situation at all. There's definitely something that goes on inside the atom and we can see its effects in different experimental situations; it isn't that I'm skeptical about there being something there. I'm skeptical about whether the language of subatomic particles is a helpful or mislead-ing way to describe it.

E: And you have the same kinds of doubts about the language about God?

F: Yes, exactly.

E: I'm beginning to understand your point, but still not very clearly.

F: Suppose someone asked you, "Do you believe your father is no longer a rapist? Yes, no, or uncertain?" How would you respond?

E: I'd respond by saying I won't answer because the question is loaded, it makes assumptions that I don't want to make.

F: Good, and you say that rather than answer "no"?

E: Sure, because the "no" answer is just as loaded as the other two.

F: Well, that's how I feel about the questions you asked me. It isn't that I don't know what I believe, it's that I don't like the "load" of your questions. So there's something wrong if I answer "yes," something wrong if I answer "no," and something wrong if I answer "uncertain."

E: So, restate the question if you don't like the way I put it.

F: If someone asked me whether God language pointed in the direction of something real and significant I'd answer "yes." If someone asked me if I thought "God exists" was a good way of describing this I'd say, "no, I don't believe it is." If someone asked me what was a good way of describing this reality I'd have to say I didn't know of any except to do it with great humility and an admission that we don't really know what we're talking about. Our language is like the cane of a blind person. It indicates that something's there but doesn't give us security about what it is.

E: So, with reference to things like electrons and God, you're like a blind man? How dismal!

F: I'd go further than that; I'd say we are all blind people. It's just that some of us have recognized it and others have not. But, unlike being blind, it doesn't have to be so tragic. It's more like gaining something than losing something.

E: So you think that nuclear physics and theology are a big mistake?

F: No, I just think they have to be done with great humility and (this may be the same thing) with an appropriate sense of humor.

E: Fred, I like you but you are truly one of the weirdest people I know. Interesting, but weird.

F: Thank you. I think that's the nicest thing you've ever said to me.

Philosophy and Language

One of the primary aims of philosophical inquiry is to become culturally aware, that is, to become aware that our thoughts, our feelings, and even our perceptions are shaped by the culture we are part of. An acute awareness of language is part of that. When we think, we think in a language, using the concepts, grammar, and rhetorical forms that language opens to us. We find it nearly impossible to think about things that our language does not name. Moreover, we find it very difficult to think about things in a way differently than our language presents them to us.

One characteristic of the English language is it is very noun focused. Our sentences tend to feature nouns and then assert things about them: "That cloud is shaped like a rabbit." Because this is the case, we are frequently tempted to think of the world as an assortment of things with certain attributes. We think of a thing, "the cloud," as having an attribute, "a shape like a rabbit." But is this a helpful way to think? Are there really such "things" as clouds? We only have to watch clouds for a little while to discover that the cloud that looks like a rabbit may become many clouds, or disappear completely, or join with others into a general cloud bank, or turn into a haze. Is there really a "thing" helpfully designated by the phrase, "that cloud"?

Would it be more accurate to use process-focused language rather than noun-focused language here? Aren't what we call clouds really just stages in a large process of evaporation and condensation? We see a cloud where the air is cool enough for the water vapor to condense and become visible.

Most of the time our noun-focused language and thing-focused way of thinking causes us little trouble. But sometimes we are lead astray by the thing/attribute approach. For a long time, for example, physicists used the language of things, subatomic *particles*, to explain the inner workings of the atom. But are there really little "things" in there, electrons, protons, mesons, and so on? Or are they all ongoing processes that we glimpse at different stages in their activity? Which way of thinking is most helpful? Which the least misleading? Are there other ways of thinking about such things that are more helpful than the thing- or process-focused approaches? It may be hard for us to think of a better model if our thinking is shaped by our conventional way of saying and conceiving things.

When anthropologists encounter other cultures it is natural for them to bring with them the categories and concepts they employed in their home culture. Someone coming from Europe a century or so ago encountering Native American cultures might have asked the question, "I wonder what god these people worship?" The question, asked in that way, might get an answer. An early explorer might have heard the Dakota make prayers to Wakan Tanka and have concluded that Wakan Tanka was the name of the Dakota's god. What these Europeans may not have realized was that the question itself already prejudiced their perceptions in a certain way. The question assumed that every culture has some equivalent to the European concept of god and that, therefore, one only has to inquire about what the name of this divinity is. On other occasions the Europeans might have heard the Dakota addressing prayers to other "divinities," and so concluded that these people were polytheists. Their conclusion assumes that the concepts, "god" and "theist" fit the new culture encountered. But a person who is culturally aware would have realized that a concept perfectly familiar in one cultural context may not fit at all well in another. The concept *kami* in Japanese, for example, is not equivalent to the Western concept "god." The Japanese would say that a particular shrine, or revered person (for example, the emperor), or a place like Mt. Fuji is *kami*. But this is not the same thing at all as claiming that each of these is a god or divine. A westerner encountering an aboriginal culture might come away thinking, "These people believe their gods live in the trees and in animals." But this may be a very mistaken way of thinking because it assumes that the concept, god, works in the aboriginal cultural context in the same way as it does in a European cultural context.

It is not easy to become culturally aware in the way we have just described. A person may have traveled around the world, experienced people from many different cultures, and still be quite blind to the fact that his own thinking is shaped by a whole bunch of assumptions. But this is precisely where philosophy begins, by noticing the concepts, categories, and forms of expression that are basic to our ways of thinking and the assumptions we make about the world because of them.

In the earlier discussion of the role of wonder in philosophy we talked briefly about the example of gravity. Because "gravity" is the right answer to the questions "Why does something thrown in the air come down?" and "Why do objects have weight?" we are encultured to believe that we understand what gravity is, and that it explains why things have weight and will fall back to earth when thrown. How do we have to look at our own language to notice that the "rightness" of the answer does not proceed very far toward advancing our understanding of the phenomena? "Gravity," after all, simply is the Latin derivative for "heaviness." How does saying that an object has heaviness explain why it has weight? It is like saying that something makes us sleepy because it is dormative or that it is sacred because it has numinosity. These may be the "right answers" in some contexts, but regarded in a slightly different way they are no answers at all. How do we have to be related to our culture, our language, and to the concepts we think with in order to notice that? How can we see past the "rightness" to see the oddity of the language?

Taking Grammar Too Seriously

Charles Lutwidge Dodgson (1832–1898), a professor of mathematics at Oxford University, wrote the popular books *Alice in Wonderland* and *Through the Looking Glass* under the pseudonym Lewis Carroll. In these books he displays an uncanny ability to notice the comical ambiguity of many phrases in the English language. Consider the following exchange between Alice and the White King in *Through the Looking Glass*:

> "I've sent them all!" the King cried in a tone of delight, on seeing Alice. "Did you happen to meet any soldiers, my dear, as you came through the wood?"
>
> "Yes, I did," said Alice: "several thousand I should think."
>
> "But I haven't sent the two Messengers. They're both gone to town. Just look along the road and tell me if you see either of them."
>
> "I see nobody on the road," said Alice.
>
> "I only wish I had such eyes," the King remarked in a fretful tone. "To be able to see Nobody! And at that distance too. Why, it's as much as I can do to see real people, by this light."
>
> At this moment the Messenger arrived: he was far too much out of breath to say a word, and could only wave his hands about, and make the most dreadful faces at the poor King.
>
> "You alarm me!" said the King. "I feel faint—Give me a ham sandwich."
>
> On which, to Alice's great amazement, the Messenger opened a bag that hung round his neck, and handed a sandwich to the King who devoured it greedily.
>
> "Another sandwich!" said the King.
>
> "There's nothing but hay left now," the Messenger said, peeping into the bag.
>
> "Hay, then," the King murmured in a faint whisper.
>
> Alice was glad to see it revived him a good deal. "There's nothing like eating hay when you're faint," he remarked to her, as he munched away.
>
> "I should think throwing cold water over you would be better," Alice suggested.

"I didn't say there was nothing better," the King replied. "I said there was nothing like it." Which Alice did not venture to deny.

"Who did you pass on the road?" the King went on.

"Nobody," said the Messenger.

"Quite right," said the King: "this young lady saw him too. So of course Nobody walks slower than you."

"I do my best," the Messenger said in a sullen tone. "I'm sure nobody walks much faster than I do."

"He can't do that," said the King, "or else he'd have been here first."

Carroll amusingly calls our attention to the difference between what the grammar of our language says (if we take it literally) and what we customarily use it to mean. Alice understands, as most of us would, the King to *mean* something different from what he literally *says*: "There's nothing like eating hay when you're faint." This should alert us to the problem of taking the grammatical structure of our language too literally. We certainly should be careful what we conclude about the world on the basis of what we say about it. The following dialogue illustrates the absurd consequences of such a mistake.

Paula: It is raining outside.

Quincy: Of course, it has to.

P: Huh? What do you mean it has to?

Q: It's much too big to be raining inside. There's not room enough for it in here.

P: Not room enough for what?

Q: For it, of course. You're the one who said, "It's raining."

P: But what is this "it" you keep referring to?

Q: Remember, you're the one who brought it up. But today it happens to be Thursday. Anyone could tell that just by looking at the calendar.

P: So you're saying that it is Thursday and it is raining outside because it's too big to be inside?

Q: Quite right. Now you're catching on.

P: Well, it's a very strange way of talking, that's for sure.

Q: Nonsense. It's not a way of talking at all. As we've already agreed, it's a day of the week and it's raining.

P: Ooh! And now it's giving me a headache.

Q: Well, you can't blame me for that.

We customarily understand that we are not referring to anything when we use the word "it" in such contexts. Thinking that every noun refers to some thing is surely a mistake. Neither "it" nor "nobody" functions that way in normal discourse.

Sometimes philosophers have been seriously misled by taking the grammar and conceptual structure of our language too literally. René Descartes, for example, wrote,

> I decided to suppose that nothing that had ever entered my mind was more real than the illusions of my dreams. But I soon noticed that while I thus wished to think everything false, it was necessarily true that I who thought so was something. Since this truth, I think therefore I am, or exist, was so firm and assured that all the most extravagant suppositions of the skeptics were unable to shake it, I judged that I could use it as the first principle of the philosophy I was seeking. (*Discourse on Method*, IV, 25)

Is Descartes being led by the grammatical necessity of the "I" in "I think" to the conclusion that there exists a thing which thinks? Descartes goes on to draw some conclusions from the fact that two concepts are distinct:

> Since I know that all the things I conceive clearly and distinctly can be produced by God exactly as I conceive them, it is sufficient that I can clearly and distinctly conceive one thing apart from another to be certain that the one is distinct from the other. For they can be made to exist separately. . . . From the very fact that I know with certainty that I exist [I think, therefore I am], and that I find that absolutely nothing else belongs necessarily to my nature or essence except that I am a thinking being, I readily conclude that my essence consists solely in being a substance whose whole essence is only to think. And although I have a body with which I am very closely united . . . since I have a clear and distinct idea of myself as a thinking and not an extended being, and since I have a distinct idea of body as an extended being which does not think, it is certain that this "I" –that is to say my soul, by virtue of which I am what I am—is entirely distinct from my body and can exist without it. (*Meditation VI*, 131–132)

What ought we conclude from the fact that two concepts are distinct, that one can be thought without thinking the other? Is it safe to conclude, as Descartes does, that the two things denoted by these concepts are separate and independent entities? Right now I am looking at a tall spruce tree out my window. The color of that tree is clearly distinct from the tree's shape. I can describe the one without talking about the other. Although I can abstract the idea of color from shape, I cannot see (or even imagine seeing) uncolored shapes or unshaped colors either. Although the concepts are distinct, they are essentially connected to each other. I see the tree's shape because it is a color distinct from the background. I see the tree's color because it has a definite shape, with edges and boundaries. Distinctiveness does not imply independence.

Thinking *About* the Concepts We Think *In*

No one finds it difficult to think *in* a language. We do it all the time. But most of us have a great deal of difficulty thinking *about* the language we think in as well as thinking about the concepts we think in terms of. Yet this is what philosophy frequently requires us to do.

In the following segment of Plato's dialogue *Meno*, we see the kind of disorientation that can occur when someone who is practiced *in* the language is required to begin thinking *about* it:

> Socrates: Answer me again from the beginning: What do you and your friend say that virtue is?
>
> Meno: Socrates, before I even met you I used to hear that you are always in a state of perplexity and that you bring others to the same state, and now I think you are bewitching me, so that I am quite perplexed. Indeed if a joke is in order, you seem both in appearance and in every other way like the broad torpedo-fish, for it too makes anyone who comes close and touches it feel numb, and you now have that effect on me, for both my mind and my tongue are numb, and I have no answer to give. Yet I have made many fine speeches about virtue before large audiences on a thousand occasions, very good speeches as I thought, but now I cannot even say what it is. (80a–b)

Meno's "many fine speeches before large audiences on a thousand occasions" have not prepared him to think *about* the concept he employs so glibly. Meno seems to have been shocked into a state of numbness by this difficulty. Other thinkers have expressed similar frustrations.

St Augustine (354–430) wrote, "What then is time? If no one asks me, I know; but if I want to explain it to a questioner, I do not know at all" (*Confessions*, XI, xiv).

Philosophy and Cultural Criticism

For some people the word *criticism* has a totally negative connotation. For them, to criticize a film, for example, means to say something negative about it. But this is only a part of the idea of criticism and not a necessary part at that. It is completely possible for someone to criticize a book, a musical performance, a play, a film, and have only praise for it. "Criticism" is not the opposite of "praise." To criticize means to evaluate based on reasons. Part of learning any art or discipline is learning what the standards and relevant reasons are for criticism in that field. Part of the responsibility of the philosopher is cultural criticism in this enlarged sense of the term.

Robert Coles gives a vivid account of his coming to a critical awareness of the concepts and categories employed by psychiatrists in diagnosing their patients. He describes his experience as a clinical intern, some of the patients he encounters, the good guidance he receives from a clinical supervisor, Dr. Ludwig, and what he learned in the whole process.

> A year into my internship, I was sitting with a young man who had attempted suicide (sleeping pills) and failed. . . .
>
> When I put that youth's "history" into a theoretical formulation, the familiar phrases appeared, none of them surprising, each of them applicable not only to that person but to many, many others: "domineering mother" (and sister), "poor masculine identification," "aloof father figure," and so on. When I named his "defenses," his "hostility," the kind of "transference" (involvement with me) he'd make, I was again consigning him (and me) to territory populated by many others. No wonder so many psychiatric reports sound banal: in each one the details of an individual life are buried under the professional jargon. We residents were learning to summon up such abstractions within minutes of seeing a patient; we directed our questions so neatly that the answers triggered the confirmatory conceptualization in our heads: a phobic, a depressive, an acting-out disorder, an identity problem, a hysterical personality.
>
> Some of those labels or categories of analysis are psychological shortcuts and don't necessarily mean offense to patients or diminishment of the user. On the other hand, the story of some

of us who become owners of a professional power and a professional vocabulary is the familiar one of moral thoughtlessness. We brandish our authority in a ceaseless effort to reassure ourselves about our importance, and we forget to look at our own warts and blemishes, so busy are we cataloguing those in others.

He [Dr. Ludwig] remarked that first-year medical students often obtain textured and subtle autobiographical accounts from patients and offer them to others with enthusiasm and pleasure, whereas fourth-year students or house officers are apt to present cryptic, dryly condensed, and, yes, all too "structured" presentations, full of abbreviations, not to mention medical or psychiatric jargon. No question: the farther one climbs the ladder of medical education the less time one has for relaxed, storytelling reflection. And patients' health may be jeopardized because of it: patients' true concerns and complaints may be overlooked as the doctor hurried to fashion a diagnosis, a procedural plan. It is not the rare patient who approaches a second doctor with the plea that he or she wasn't heard, that the first physician had his or her mind made up from the start of a consultation and went ahead accordingly with a diagnostic and therapeutic regimen.

All too commonly . . . some of us use theory more as a badge of membership than as a visual stimulus. We might use ideas in such a manner as to make us eagle-eyed; instead, often enough, we see as sheep do. Moreover, we keep saying certain words out loud, as tokens of loyalty in the company of our colleagues, and repeat them silently while we hear patients tell us not only what has brought them to us, but what they hope to gain from us. Under such circumstances, they may get what they had not bargained for—an indoctrination. As for us, the doctors, we get further confirmation of the correctness of what we resolutely believe. (*The Call of Stories*, 17–21)

Practitioners in all areas need to be open, as Coles was, to seeing how the use of an established vocabulary may blind them to aspects of reality that do not fit their categorical schemes. There is certainly more than one kind of blindness. Philosophy, considered as a critique of abstractions, is a kind of therapy for such blindness, an attempt to once again see what has been in plain view all along.

Questions for Further Reflection

1. The opening dialogue suggests that sometimes questions can bring an agenda with them and establish a limited set of things that are

available as answers. Can you give other examples of such "questions with an agenda"? How do the questions we ask shape our thinking toward an answer?

2. The dialogue also contrasts two kinds of doubt. How would you characterize these two kinds and how are they different? In what contexts do you feel most confident in the adequacy of language? Where do you feel the least confident? Why?

3. The text suggests that sometimes, at least, process-focused language serves better than thing- focused language. Can you think of other areas of experience where this might be the case? How else might language be focused than in these two ways? Can learning a substantially different language open our eyes to new aspects of reality? Interview someone who is learning a significantly different language (e.g., Chinese, Swahili, Hebrew) to see what they have discovered.

4. The discussion of Descartes suggests that he was led by the grammar of language into positing "a thinking thing" separate from his body. Is there an alternative way to understand Descartes's inference? If we should not infer what Descartes did about the existence and nature of this "I," what should we conclude about it? (See Chapter Seven for further discussion of this issue.)

5. The selection from *Through the Looking Glass* illustrates the kinds of problems that can arise if we take the grammar of our language too seriously. Can you think of other (more serious) examples where this seems to be the problem? Friedrich Nietzsche (see Chapter Seven) suggests that both the concept of the self and the concept of God are grammatical mistakes.

6. Robert Coles clearly illustrates the process of discovering how much damage a set vocabulary and a set of established categories can do. What are some other areas besides psychology where this may take place? Does Coles suggest an alternative approach? What might be changed in the education of psychiatrists to help avoid such a problem?

7. A.N. Whitehead considers an abstraction to be "a name or a category mistaken for reality." Friedrich Nietzsche similarly argued that we frequently, "care more what something is called than what it is." Where, in our patterns of thinking, do we make these kinds of mistakes? See if you can find at least three different kinds of examples. What do we learn about ourselves when we discover this misplaced allegiance?

Works Cited

Augustine. *Confessions*, trans. J.G. Pilkington. New York: Liveright & Co., 1943.

Carroll, Lewis (Charles Lutwidge Dodgson). *Through the Looking Glass,* in *The Complete Works of Lewis Carroll.* New York: Random House/ Modern Library, 1982.

Coles, Robert. *The Call of Stories: Teaching and the Moral Imagination.* Boston: Houghton Mifflin, 1989.

Descartes, René. *Discourse on Method* and *Meditations*, trans. L.J. Lafleur. New York: Macmillan/Library of Liberal Arts, 1960.

Plato. *Meno*, trans. G.M.A. Grube. Indianapolis: Hackett, 1976.

CHAPTER SIX

Freedom and Self-Determination

This chapter explores the nature of human freedom. The dialogue raises many of the main questions on the topic. The discussion that follows distinguishes three senses of freedom: political, metaphysical, and practical. The rest of the chapter focuses on practical freedom, seeking to understand what it is and what we may do to increase it.

Dialogue VI

Jay: So how would you guys answer the question that came up in class: What is freedom?

Kay: That's easy. Freedom is doing what you want. You know, like not having someone who tells you that you can't.

J: So a drug addict who had an adequate supply of drugs and had nobody to tell him that he can't use them would be free?

Lila: No way! An addict is not free, he's controlled.

J: But he does what he wants, right?

L: No, I don't think so. He does what he thinks he wants, but he doesn't do what he really wants because he's controlled by the addiction.

K: Yeah, but how can you tell the difference? I mean what's the difference between wanting and really wanting? Can the addict tell the difference?

May: I think some can. People may be controlled by something and know they are, but not like it. So in a sense they want the thing that controls them and in a sense they don't.

K: You mean they have wants they don't want? That seems like a funny way to talk.

M: Yes, but sometimes we have to say funny things to reflect the way things are.

J: So how should we revise the initial definition, "Freedom is doing what you want?"

L: I'd say, "Freedom is wanting what you *really* want."

K: Hmm, but then I think maybe freedom is impossible.

M: Why?

K: I don't think we know what we really want. I mean, we live in a culture that's constantly telling us what we should want. Ads say, "You want to be beautiful, sexy, sophisticated, cool, so you want this car, or these jeans, or these sneakers, or this deodorant." Our friends tell us what to be like, and our parents, and everybody who is selling something. Ads even try to sell you on the idea that freedom is owning a Jeep or something that you can drive anywhere with. "Don't let the road hold you back." You know that ad? How can you help but want all the stuff you're being sold? So I think if freedom is knowing what you really want, then it's impossible. I sure don't know what I really want, but I know that I want a lot of the stuff they're trying to sell me. We're like puppets. Somebody is always pulling our strings.

J: Isn't there some way to avoid being controlled in this way?

M: Yes. I still think that you're not controlled if you know what you really want.

K: But how can you tell it's really you and your real wants and not just somebody pulling your strings?

L: I notice that advertising isn't usually about the stuff they're selling, it's about us. It works to control the actions of millions of people because the ad people know how dependent we are on other's telling us we're OK. The real me is sometimes pretty scared and unsure. Maybe the real me wants to be lead by the nose.

J: Because basically we believe that we're nobody without neat stuff. Just try to get a cool date without a neat car.

M: So do you want a girl to like you or to like your car?

J: In most cases it seems like the same thing. If my car is cool then I'm cool. Isn't that your experience?

M: I don't agree. A person who's liked only for what they *have* isn't being liked for who they *are*. I don't think it's hard to tell the difference. Some people who have lots of stuff are nobodies.

J: I disagree. Don't we all know that's how you really get to be somebody?

M: I don't agree at all. Having and being are not the same thing.

K: Well. I want to know whether you think we've made a step toward freedom by just thinking about the things we've been talking about.

L: No, not if we're still controlled, and most people are to a very large degree.

K: I think I may have made a step, because now I'm thinking about it and before I wasn't. But it's not a very big step. It's like I'm still the puppet but now I know I am. I see the strings. I now just feel kind of stupid for wanting the stuff I want because I know I'm being jerked around. But I still don't know how to get to freedom—though I guess I realize it has something to do with knowing who I am.

K: You know, I really dislike questions like this. They leave me more confused than I was before. If the question hadn't been posed we'd just be going on our merry way, supposing that we're free and that we know what we want and who we are.

M: Just because you don't think about the question doesn't mean that you know the answer.

L: Yeah. There's some truth in the saying that ignorance is bliss.

M: Yes, but it's still ignorance.

L: I think knowledge is overrated, particularly knowledge that leaves us frustrated. It's like the story my dad tells:

A guy says, "I learned from watching the news that cigarette smoking can cause cancer."

His friend asks, "So have you decided to quit smoking?"

The guy responds, "Hell no. I decided to quit watching the news."

Three Senses of "Freedom"

There are at least three distinguishable ways of talking about freedom, based roughly on three different things we wish to contrast freedom with. Perhaps that means there are different kinds of freedom and not all talk about this subject is talk about the same thing.

1. The first sense is **political freedom**, that is, what a citizen enjoys in a country where he or she gets to vote, can publicly express opinions contrary to those held by persons in power, can participate in a political party of choice, and can pursue the religious or other beliefs and practices one chooses. This freedom also frequently goes by the name "liberty" and is the focus of much political activity and rhetoric around the world. Such **freedom is contrasted to tyranny or other forms of totalitarianism.** An analysis of the rhetoric of political freedom would require several book-length works by itself.

2. The second sense of freedom does not have a common name, but we refer to it as **metaphysical freedom**. It is the sort of freedom philosophers (and others) talk about when they debate about **freedom vs. determinism**. Determinism is the view that every event is the predictable result of causes that precede it. These causes, therefore, "determine" what will occur next. Our behavior and our choices, being events in the world, are thus said to be determined by antecedent conditions. Whatever happens, by this view, happens by causal necessity. Any talk of freedom of action or freedom of will is, according to the determinist, either false or completely superfluous. To argue for freedom, on the other hand, is usually to assert either that determinism is not true or that it is, at least, not the whole truth.

A thorough discussion of such arguments could also occupy several volumes. But there are a few things we should be aware of in this debate. Both sides in the freedom vs. determinism debate seem to assume that an event's being caused implies it is determined. That assumption may have been warranted given some older ideas of causality, but it doesn't seem necessary given more recent scientific ideas such as "indeterminacy" and "chaos theory." These theories suggest that it may be possible to talk about causality as having a kind of statistical predictability without really "determining" the future.

Both sides also seem to assume that for an action to be free it must be, in some sense, uncaused, that is, causally disconnected from the conditions that precede it. But even a little reflection shows that this is not what we usually mean by freedom. Isn't a free action *self-caused* rather than *uncaused*? Do we even have any clear conception of what an "uncaused action" would be like? Would we suddenly discover our body doing things at random, things we hadn't planned, or even thought about doing? Would it make sense to refer to such events as an action at all? These are only a couple of the many questions that a complete discussion of this issue must include, but they may be sufficient to show that this debate, as it stands, is very confused. The philosopher's role here should be to attempt to clarify the confusion rather than to weigh in on one side or the other. This is, I believe, an example of a philosophical issue that begins by framing the question in the wrong way (see Chapter Eight).

3. The third type of freedom we call **practical freedom.** This is the freedom we exercise when we make daily personal choices. It is the sort of freedom we seek when we wish to act beyond the control or manipulation of others. This is the freedom the participants in the dialogue **contrasted to "having our strings pulled."** In the discussion that follows we critically examine some commonly voiced views of practical freedom. We conclude by offering some strategies for increasing freedom together with some illustrative examples.

Some Common Characterizations of Practical Freedom

"Freedom is being able to make a choice." We often assume that freedom is guaranteed by our being able to make a choice. When we walk down the cereal aisle in a supermarket we are confronted with hundreds of choices. We only have to decide what kind, flavor, shape, color, and brand we want to buy. Surely this is the epitome of freedom, isn't it?

My seven-year-old daughter walks down that aisle with me. She makes her choice. "I want this one," she says, plopping the brightly colored box into our shopping cart. Is her freedom guaranteed by the fact that she made a choice? Was it increased by the fact that she had so many choices she could have made? I think the answer to both questions is negative. Why? In the first place, it is possible that her choice was itself manipulated by someone else. Did she choose the cereal because of the ad she saw on TV earlier that morning? Did she buy it because of the cartoon character who appears on the box? Or was it the Barbie doll advertised on the back? One is not freed by making a choice if the choice is itself manipulated by others. The question of freedom must be chased back further. We cannot stop with asking, "Did I have a choice?" We also need to ask, "Was I manipulated into choosing as I did?" Second, the number of choices available has little to do with freedom. I can freely choose from a menu of two items if one of them is something I really want. Having a hundred more items available doesn't by itself increase my freedom. It may increase the probability that I'll find something I like, but it's no guarantee. Freedom seems to lie in my relationship to the choice, not in the scope or variety of the things that may be chosen.

Very similar to the conception just considered is the view that **"freedom is proportional to our possibilities."** I recently took my son to the music store. He had outgrown his violin and was ready to move up a size. While he was trying out a new instrument, a woman, accompanied by a daughter who was about my son's age, asked me, "How long has your son been playing the violin?" I said, "Since he was four years old, he's now eleven." After a pause I asked, "Does your daughter play an instrument?" The mother replied, "I'd like her to play something. We stop in here every couple of months and look at all the instruments. I want her to have freedom of choice, so for right now, we're keeping our options open."

This conversation made me stop and think, "Did I limit my son's freedom by getting him started on violin so early?" Should we have kept more options open? Doesn't the possibility of playing tuba or banjo or saxophone or drums increase one's freedom? Wouldn't a person who had the possibility of playing all those things be freer than the person who only knew how to play one? It is tempting to think so, but I don't think it's true.

My son is now free to do something that the woman's daughter is not: he is free to play the violin right now at a fairly advanced level and make some nice music doing so. He plays in his school chamber orchestra and he has performed in public several times. Thus the contrast is between freedom considered theoretically and freedom actualized. Does actualizing one possibility make one more or less free than merely considering many possibilities? Am I more free before I order from a menu than after I order? After I order I'm "stuck" with what I ordered. Wasn't I more free before? Theoretically it seems so. Yet I can't eat a merely theoretical lunch.

I have heard some parents say, "I don't want to push things on my kids." The context for this remark is usually talk about morality or religious beliefs or political views. "When they grow up they can consider all the possibilities and choose from among them." This sounds like considerate and enlightened parenting, but on examination there also seems to be something strangely unrealistic about it. Can one really present an eighteen-year-old with, say, the variety of the world's religions and meaningfully say, "Choose one, dear. Have you considered becoming a Sufi or a Zoroastrian?"

Freedom is related not so much to theoretical possibilities as it is to things that are realistically actualizable for me. Something may be a theoretical possibility that is not really a live option. That I can actually converse in three languages makes me, I believe, more free than having the *possibility* of conversing in hundreds. Someone might ask, "But why would you limit yourself that way?" My response would be that no list of possibilities, no matter how large, can outweigh one actuality.

Another commonly voiced view supposes that **"freedom is getting rid of external influences."** Personal freedom is certainly inconsistent with being controlled by someone else. To a lesser extent, it is inconsistent with being coerced and manipulated by others. So we might suppose that being influenced by others is just a slightly milder form of control and coercion. Sometimes we suppose that the free person is some kind of wilderness loner, living without society, without a boss, without family or neighbors, and certainly without TV or advertising. Is that an adequate image of freedom?

Imagine a situation where people I respect have given me advice. Because I respect them, I will probably take their advice seriously, weighing it carefully in my deliberations. It may be that it is very good advice they have given me, and I see that it is. Am I acting freely if I do what they suggest? Or does freedom require that I reject all such advice as being "an outside influence"? Isn't it the case that the original source of the idea that we act on is quite irrelevant to the issue of freedom? If I get my plan of action from a respected friend, or from an enemy, or from a song I heard on the radio, or from a matchbook cover, what has that to do with the issue of freedom? Freedom seems to be a function not of the source of the idea, but with the fact that I have made it *my* plan, *my* intention, *the action that I really want to pursue*. So, it seems, the idea that freedom means to be beyond influence misplaces the issue of freedom. It sees as external a problem that really is internal.

I frequently hear students say **"freedom would be increased if we didn't have any rules or restrictions."** This might be called an anarchist's view of freedom, the view that it's society's rules which infringe on our autonomy. Although it's possible this is so, it's also possible that rules (and rulers) enable freedom. Members of an orchestra may follow the program, tempo and interpretation set by their conductor. Doing so limits their individual freedom. They are not free to begin and end when they wish, nor to play any piece they wish, any way they wish. Yet the presence and work of the conductor enables another freedom, namely the freedom of being a symphony orchestra playing a particular piece of music. We must not neglect the things we are **freed to** do in our thinking about freedom. And we should be aware of the temptation to think of freedom solely as a **freedom from** the influence of others. Freedom is not always manifest in breaking or getting rid of rules or rulers, for that matter. So the anarchist's view reflects only a fraction of the reality of freedom.

Some Tentative Conclusions

What have we learned about freedom from articulating and critiquing these views? I offer four conclusions: (1) Although choosing may be a manifestation of freedom, the presence of choice does not necessitate the presence of freedom. My choices may themselves be so thoroughly manipulated by others that they are not genuinely mine at all. It does me no good to get what I choose if I am not free to choose what I choose. Moreover, I may act freely even where I have little choice, provided that I am doing what I truly want to do. So choice is not a sufficient condition of freedom, and it may not even be a necessary one. (2) Freedom is not necessarily proportional to theoretical possibilities, although it is related to actualizable realities. The development of actual skills and abilities may increase our freedom in ways that the mere presence of possibilities do not. (3) Freedom is not the same as being non-influenced. Instead freedom is proportional to our ability to recognize and evaluate influences adequately. (4) Freedom has little to do with what happens to be the source of the idea or plan we act on. On the other hand, it has much to do with whether the action I am performing is really mine, that is, whether I identify with it and see it as an expression of my inmost identity.

The title of this section is "Some Tentative Conclusions." You may ask, "If those are your conclusions, why do you offer them tentatively?" The reason is that all of them rest on an assumption we have not yet explicitly examined: that all of this talk about what "I really want," an action that is "really mine," that is an expression of my "inmost identity," makes sense. If we really cannot distinguish such actions from actions that are controlled or manipulated by others, then all this talk about freedom is ill advised. Is there any way to advance our understanding on this issue?

In regard to practical freedom we are never completely free, nor are we ever completely without freedom. We are always somewhere in the middle continuum of more or less. Practical freedom (and its absence) are not absolute states of affairs. So we can never say absolutely, "This is a case of complete freedom," or "This is a case of complete loss of freedom." So, although the distinction between freedom and nonfreedom is not absolute, that does not imply it is not a distinction which cannot be meaningfully made. I think we can distinguish the cases of more freedom from those with less, and in many cases we can state what, in the situation, might increase our freedom. There are many examples that witness this is so.

We can become more (as well as less) free in any situation, and interestingly I believe, we have some degree of freedom over how free we want to be. The degree of our practical freedom is something that we can do something about. The following strategies (and the accompanying examples) are offered not only to detail how we might increase our freedom. They are also offered as evidence that this distinction between more and less freedom can be meaningfully made in a practical way. If they work to affect the former, then they are evidence that talk about actions that are "really mine," and that "express my identity," makes a real and applicable distinction.

Increasing Our Freedom: Six Strategies with Examples

Strategy 1. We may increase our freedom by becoming more aware of the means other people use to control us. Like the students in the opening dialogue, we can, with a little reflection, become aware of the ways other people (whether intentionally or not) and things "pull our strings."

> **Example:** A young woman says, "Sometimes my mother drives me crazy. She treats me like a child and consequently I behave like a child in response and then she feels justified in treating me like a child, and so the cycle continues. Our time together is awful."

How can we help this young woman (and her mother) avoid getting into this frustrating pattern? The first bit of advice might be to say, "Become aware of what it is the other person says or does that sets you off. If you can be aware of it, perhaps you can avoid responding to it so automatically. When you, and not the other person, start to influence your responses you're a step on your way to increased freedom." If we recognize the stimulus we may be less automatic with the response. The more our actions are mere responses to stimuli the less deliberate they are; and the less deliberate, the less free.

Less than 20 percent of car buyers actually research or think through their auto purchases. Less than 35 percent bother to get a comparative price on the car they are buying. Most people make such purchases as "reaction buyers," responding to the immediate aesthetic appeal of the car and their image of themselves in it. Auto sales agents help the buyers "imagine themselves behind the wheel," and "imagine the reactions of your friends." Few actually help us think through what our car needs are, what our priorities are, and what price we are willing to pay for these things. A survey of car buyers one year after purchase usually turns up many responses like these: "I bought more car than I really needed," "I bought one of those sport utility vehicles and I hardly ever use that space. I guess I was just impressed by how big it was and how powerful it seemed." "I ended up paying a lot for styling. Now the new models make mine look out of style, but I can't sell it after just a year and still get for it what I still owe. The first year's payments are almost all interest."

How can we help consumers become better at buying what they really want? The first step is for us to become aware of the way our "strings are pulled." Only if we become conscious of the appeal certain features have for us, or the way certain ads make us feel, will we have a chance of resisting them and moving toward our own freedom. I have a friend who helps herself control her compulsive shopping by asking herself over and over, "What is it *about me* that makes me think I need this thing so desperately?" She says that voicing this makes her focus on herself and not on the glitzy thing she was about to buy. "Then I'm able to walk away from it and feel good about myself for doing so."

Strategy 2. We may increase our freedom when we begin to realize where our own ideas and assumptions have come from. Where did we get our ideas about what's in or out of fashion? Where did we get the definitions of success that dominate and drive us? Where did we get the assumptions we make about which people are "cool" and which are "out of it"? These ideas and attitudes did not come out of thin air. All of them have a history and a source. We increase our freedom as we increase our consciousness of the sources of our own ways of thinking.

> **Example:** A sixteen-year-old girl gets arrested and convicted for shoplifting. It's her third conviction. She explains to her attorney and the court-appointed social worker why she has been doing this since she was thirteen: "You're completely nobody if you don't have neat stuff. I mean, if you're not wearing the *right* brands you are really out of it. You're *nobody*. I mean, people won't even talk to you. They won't even *see you*. If you've got rich parents you're lucky. I take this stuff because I need it, don't you see?"

If we asked this girl where she got her ideas of what are "neat stuff" and the "right brands" she'd probably say that she learns these things from advertising and from her friends. The pressure to conform comes from them. But where did her peers get the idea that's been communicated so clearly to her, namely that without neat stuff a person is truly a nobody? Where did they get the impression that "neat stuff" and the "right brands" make them all somebody? Who is informing them of this? Most of the messages we get in our society about what it means to be a successful, substantial, fulfilled human being come from people who are trying to sell us something. When these messages are reinforced by the preferences and consumption patterns of parents, kids (as well as adults) find it very difficult not to be controlled by them.

Realizing that we are being "sold" not just a product but also an image of ourselves may not by itself be fully liberating, but it is a step toward freedom. Once we realize that our ideas and assumptions have a source, that they are not simply "given," we are in a position to begin to question them. As long as they simply seem to be the way "everybody" thinks, we question neither their source nor their validity.

Strategy 3. We increase our freedom when we know or can imagine viable alternatives to the ways things are presented to us. The power of imagination allows us to ask, "Why do we do things the way we do?" and "Why don't we do it another way?" When it occurs to us to ask, we may be in a position to hear how feeble the reasons are that we give to defend the status quo (e.g., "That's how we've always done it," or "That's how right-thinking people do it").

Example: A businessman was urged by his banker to hire a consultant to find out why productivity had been declining in his company. He explained to the consultant at the outset, "I don't see why productivity and profits are lower now than they used to be. We're doing things exactly the same now as we used to do them when my father was in charge, and productivity was much higher. This is the way we've always done it. What could be wrong with that?" What the consultant did was bring in a fresh view, without any loyalty or commitment to "the way we've always done it," and a knowledge of some alternatives. Her experience of the way things work in a variety of companies freed her to find the problems in the company under study. She repeatedly asked the employees of the company to answer two questions: "What are you trying to accomplish here?" and "What's the most efficient way to do that?" This critical questioning made them rethink the way they had been doing things and to imagine alternatives. Her final report recommended three alternative ways of reorganizing the business. She left it to the owner to make the final decision. What she had done was increase his (and his employees') freedom by enabling their imaginations and loosening the hold the established pattern had over them. Only then could they actually consider and evaluate alternative ways of doing things.

Strategy 4. We increase our freedom when we are able to question effectively and critique reliably those assumptions and ideas that most thoroughly "pull our strings." We move toward freedom not only when we realize the power that images, assumptions, ideas, and arguments have over us, but when we can come to question and evaluate the adequacy of these things.

Half of this strategy is the posing of crucial questions: Is the "Marlboro man" the image of what "a real man" looks like? Does successful maleness or femaleness follow only one pattern? Why should possessions determine whether one is a somebody or a nobody? We increase our freedom not merely through the posing of such questions but through coming, through practice, to trust our own abilities at critical reasoning and decision making.

People lack the power to question and critique basic assumptions they make (1) because they don't see them as assumptions at all but see them as necessities, "just the way things are," and/or (2) because they haven't seriously considered any alternatives, and/or (3) because they have been well trained to never question the authority of some power group, whether parents, bosses, a peer group, or society as a whole, and/or (4) because they have not developed their powers of critical reasoning.

> **Examples:** A student accompanied her roommate to a political rally and next day she reported to an old friend that the rally had completely changed her views on politics. But after a brief conversation with her friend she changed her mind again, now agreeing with her friend's political views. In an essay she wrote, "It's as though I agree with the last person I talked to or the last argument I read. I know it's good to be open-minded and to hear different views, but I don't seem to be able to sort things out. As a consequence, I don't have a mind of my own. Like a weather vane, I point whatever direction the wind happens to be blowing at the time."
>
> A middle-aged man has a clearly delineated set of beliefs and values that he is convinced are correct. He is so devoted to these

views that he refuses to hear or read alternative points of view. Not only does he not seek them out, he will turn off the radio or TV if he encounters a program with a view different from his own. Many times he has walked away from conversations in which a person has offered a view different from his own.

These two examples seem like opposites, so we might be inclined to think that because one of them lacks freedom, the opposite must be a fine example of freedom. But in this case both of these extremes fail to exhibit much freedom. The former example shows us a young woman who is completely malleable to outside influences. The latter shows us a man who is so rigid and close-minded that he will not even hear an alternative. The former person can not sort out the voices she hears and thus is influenced equally by all of them. The latter person refuses to hear any other voice than his own.

What the persons in both of these examples have in common is a mistrust of their own critical intelligence. The woman lacks an ability to critique and evaluate the voices she hears. Consequently, she believes the last person to talk to her. The man refuses to hear (perhaps because he is afraid to hear) alternative views. Mistrusting his critical abilities he simply shuts out things he doesn't agree with. In neither example do we have a person who considers alternatives and then critically evaluates them. Both of them are focused merely on whether they agree or disagree, not on the process of critical reasoning that would be required to sort out good arguments from bad, strong evidence from weak, and so on. The man is threatened by opposing views because he may feel himself defenseless to them. Like the young woman, he is one step away from believing everything he hears and consequently fears to hear anything different. Freedom would be greater for both of these people if they enhanced and came to trust their own powers of critical evaluation. An increase in critical intelligence could lead, in both their cases, to increased personal freedom.

Strategy 5. We may increase our freedom when we can plan and prioritize our lives for the long term and can actualize the skills and self-discipline necessary to act on such plans. Addicts or people with an insatiable habit may initially feel good when they do what they immediately desire. What they are not free to do is to control their immediate desires so as to act for a larger or longer range good. The student who uses self-discipline and can budget her time well has more freedom than the student who immediately satisfies every passing whim. The person with self-control has more freedom than the person who is controlled by his immediate desires. The self-disciplined person can do things that the compelled person simply cannot manage.

The prudent person, that is, the person who can act on long-range, enlightened self interest, is more free than the person driven by immediate desires. The moral person, that is, the person who can evaluate his actions in a larger transpersonal context, is more free than the egotist. The political person (in the classical sense of political, i.e., a person who can evaluate her own actions in terms of the common good) is more free than the person who knows only what serves herself. In each of these cases we move toward freedom as we move toward seeing our actions in a larger, longer, more inclusive context.

> **Example:** A ninth grade boy uses all his free time reading stories about sports heroes and watching sports on TV. His time in school is spent daydreaming about becoming a sports hero himself, hitting the game-winning run, scoring the winning basket, competing in the Olympics. Meanwhile, he does not try out for any school sports, nor does he get high enough grades to be eligible even if he did. The less he accomplishes in his actual life, the more he retreats into his rich fantasy life. There he accomplishes great things, wins games, is admired for what he does. When his family finally buys a computer he "loses himself" in virtual reality sports for hours every day. During these same years another boy in the neighborhood sets himself the discipline (beginning in fifth grade) to shoot 100 jump shots every day at the neighborhood basketball court. His skills continually improve and he is able to make the varsity team both at his high school and in college.

We often suppose that the most free person is the most uncommitted and undisciplined, the person who is "free as a bird." It is hard for us to imagine that freedom often requires focused effort *and discipline*. I am not free to use a language until I have made the considerable effort to learn it. I am not free to play the cello or be a competitive gymnast unless I am willing to put in the hours of practice necessary to master it. I am not free to write computer software until I have mastered the knowledge and skills needed to do so. I am not free to become an attorney until I have put in the years of study necessary to do so. Are the people who are so hard at work doing such things increasing their freedom? Yes, in fact they are. Commitment, effort, and self-discipline are frequently the necessary ingredients for increased freedom. How commonly we assume the exact opposite.

Strategy 6. *We increase our freedom when we start to shape the things we are shaped by.* Our culture shapes us, our social and political system shapes us, our educational system shapes us. All of these things have no small influence on the ways we think, the things we value, and the ways we act. We may increase our freedom when we, in turn, become active in shaping culture, society, politics, the educational system, and so on. A lot of people feel that politics, for example, is something that some impersonal "they" do to "us." In a democracy, of course, each of us has the possibility to become actively involved, overcome the alienating hurdle between us and them, and make an effort to change things for the better. Many people think about morality as a set of rules pushed on us by some anonymous authority called "society." But who are "they"? Who makes up "society"? We are never uninfluenced, but we can, with attention and effort, also become persons of influence. We can begin to shape influential agendas and not just be shaped by them.

> **Example:** A small group of concerned parents organized a Web site to talk about the negative influences of violent TV on their children. They soon found that hundreds of thousands of people across the nation were signing on weekly to their Web site. They organized to write letters to the sponsors of the most offensive programs and sent copies to the networks and local TV stations. They have now become a national organization called "The Caring Parents TV Network." A little bit at a time they are changing the menu of offerings during kids' TV-watching hours. Some companies now regularly consult with them before deciding what programs they will sponsor. They have become an influence in the TV market; they are no longer merely influenced by it.

Summary Thoughts

Have you ever met anyone who is happy to think of himself or herself as a puppet whose strings are constantly being pulled by others? Most of us, it seems to me, want to think of ourselves as free and responsible. Yet there are people who strongly resist any effort to help them think about who and what controls them, or who resent any effort to help them be more reflective about these influences. Some of the limited and controlled people in our examples may be very firmly set in the illusion that binds them. They may have come, in some cases, to love their "addiction" more than their freedom. Thus, even though we may offer strategies for increased freedom, we should not be surprised if people resist actualizing them. Increasing freedom, like increasing our awareness of reality, frequently takes courage as well as effort and discipline.

The students in the opening dialogue discovered that practical freedom is a multilayered problem. As soon as we think we have solved it at one level, it seems to reoccur at another level. We may be free to act as we choose, yet have our choices limited and/or manipulated by others. We may be free to choose, but have the thinking that informs our choices severely limited and/or controlled. We may have different points of view open to us yet be unable to sort them out in a critical way. We may choose, yet be strongly influenced in our choice by things we aren't even aware of, and consequently do not influence ourselves.

In summary, freedom is connected to knowing what the influences as well as the options are, having reason to trust our own critical intelligence, "having a mind of our own," and knowing why we think as we do about important things. Freedom is connected, in other words, to critical awareness, self-knowledge, identity, deliberateness, and reflectiveness.

One of the most helpful and provocative discussions of freedom I have read is by Frithjof Bergmann in his book, *On Being Free*. There Bergmann argues that freedom is not so much a struggle against external restraints as it is the finding and expressing of an inner identity. The prerequisite of freedom is to have a self that wants to be expressed in action. Bergmann writes,

> Freedom is a function of identification, not choice . . . (78).
> The problem of freedom is in large part the problem of how to keep the self alive, how to devise a mode of education and a society which do not extinguish it. . . . What renders a man unfree is therefore not constraints—these are inevitable—but the increasing distance from, and the eventual loss of a foundation in himself. (97)

Thomas Merton said that freedom is not merely choice, but "Choosing the chooser who chooses" (4). This may be another way of stating the point that Bergmann is making.

If Bergmann and Merton are right about this, it means the discussion of freedom leads us necessarily to an inquiry about the self and identity. So that is what we investigate in Chapter Seven.

Questions for Further Reflection

1. The first definition of freedom that comes up in the opening dialogue is "doing what you want." Why is that such a natural and tempting answer? Try asking your own acquaintances to define freedom and

see how many initially say much the same thing. Do people in other cultures see freedom differently? Do people tend to see the issues of freedom differently at different stages of life? Conduct some interviews and see what you find out.

2. May argues in the dialogue that a person who is liked for *what he has* is not liked for *who he is*. Jay seems inclined to think that these are much the same thing. What do you think? Can possessions make us *be* somebody? Is a person without cool things really a nobody as the girl states in the example connected to strategy 2?

3. How are the three senses of "freedom" related to each other? Are they really different kinds of freedom, or are they the same thing seen in different aspects? If they are different, which is the most crucial? Are some of these kinds or senses of freedom dependent on each other?

4. Why are sport utility vehicles now so popular? What message do they convey to their owners? How do they make them feel about themselves? Is this feeling changed by realizing that most SUV owners use them to commute from their suburban homes to their offices?

5. Strategy 6 implies that becoming more prudent, and becoming more morally and politically engaged and more committed, actually increases our freedom. Can this really be true? Why does this conflict with the way many of us tend to think about freedom?

6. People sometimes strongly resist attempts to help them move toward their own freedom. Can you think of an example of this? Why should this be the case? Aren't freedom and self-determination things that everyone desires for themselves?

7. Does education have anything to do with freedom? Are there some kinds of learning that have more to do with it than others? Could there ever be a liberating curriculum?

Works Cited

Bergmann, Frithjoff. *On Being Free.* Notre Dame: University of Notre Dame Press, 1977.

Merton, Thomas. "Learning to Live," in *Love and Living.* New York: Bantam Books, 1979.

CHAPTER SEVEN

The Search for the Authentic Self

This chapter explores four theories of the human self: by Aristotle, Nietzsche, Sartre, and de Beauvoir, plus some illustrations from fiction and drama. Do we have an essential human self, or is there a vacuum at the center? Which view supports freedom—the idea of an essential self or the idea that there is none?

Dialogue VII

Jay: I've been thinking some more about freedom since we talked about it yesterday. We said something about the necessity to know who you really are and not just listen to somebody else tell you who you are.

Kay: Yes, I remember saying something like that.

J: Well, I don't see how we can ever know who we really are. In order to choose freely I've got to choose what I really want. But how do I ever know my wants are really mine? I can be made to want something by seeing a TV ad for it. In order to act freely it seems that I have to know my own deepest wants, to know what is really in my self-interest.

K: And you think that we can't know what's really in our self-interest?

J: Well, I'm not sure, but I have a lot of doubts about it.

Lila: Yes, I think I understand what you mean. Right now in some part of the world there is some war going on based on a history of racial or ethnic hatred. Those guys are out there killing each other off because they believe that eliminating each other is in their own group's self-interest. They're willing to base their lives and risk their necks on it, they're that sure it's true. But it seems to me they are really very mistaken. That's the way they grew up thinking, so it's very hard for them to imagine anything else. I doubt they are really free to think otherwise.

J: Yeah, that's a good example.

K: But there's something about that situation that makes us doubt that is really their self-interest.

J: Yes, so?

K: So it isn't impossible to see past such a mistake. It may be difficult to overcome a set of beliefs you grew up with, but that doesn't mean it's impossible. We sometimes realize we've been jerked around by others, or that we've been thinking in prejudiced ways, or that we've been working on a false assumption. Illusions are hard to shed but not impossible. So you may be right in noticing the difficulty of self-knowledge, but wrong in concluding that it's impossible.

J: But is there anything besides just layers of illusions? You're assuming that if you can shed an illusion you get closer to the kernel of truth. But maybe we're like onions and there's no real self to know once we get in there. If there's no core self then I don't suppose there's such a thing as my "real self-interest" either.

L: This talk about "real self" and "real self-interest" sort of scares me. Imagine people coming into a culture and persuading them that the way they've always been doing things is wrong because it doesn't accord with their "real self-interest." The natives are surprised to hear this because they've assumed all along that their self-interest was what they were pursuing. But now they come to doubt their old ways and start chasing what they're told is their self-interest. Do you see the danger of talking that way?

J: I think of missionaries when you say that.

K: I think of modern Western economists. I think they've persuaded more people to abandon their traditional cultural wisdom than any missionaries were ever able to do. They've persuaded a lot of people that they're not really happy if they're not part of the consumer culture.

L: Both are good examples. Both rely on making people mistrust their native culture and traditions in order to be persuasive.

K: But in some cases, like the ethnic hatred and violence example, people might be better off shedding such traditions even if it's a deep part of their history and culture. The citizens of Massachusetts used to burn witches, but I don't hear anyone suggesting that it's too bad we lost that part of our "native culture."

L: Think of the example of women. For centuries they have been persuaded to accept secondary roles in society on the grounds that they had a different "essential nature" from men. Women, for example, were denied educational opportunity and the right to vote on the grounds that they were not rational but emotional creatures. It's things like this that make me suspicious when people start talking about our "real self" and "real self-interest."

J: But the argument also runs the other way, doesn't it?

L: How do you mean?

J: Suppose we lived in a society that told us we couldn't do something or had to do something on the grounds that this was in accord with our real nature. Suppose also that we didn't agree and that we wanted to rebel against this image of ourselves that society had handed us.

L: Yes, I follow you so far.

J: On what grounds could we make such an argument? Wouldn't we want to argue that the society had no right to treat us as slaves or put us in secondary roles because it was contrary to our true nature as human beings?

K: Isn't that what the Bill of Rights of our Constitution argued? That we had "certain inalienable rights" just because of our nature as human beings?

L: So what we discover is that we need language about "the real self" and "real self-interest" and that such language can be used for both good and ill.

K: It's just like every other sort of language in that respect.

J: So where does that leave us?

L: I'd say it leaves us realizing how important and difficult it is to have the self-knowledge necessary for freedom.

May: So what are you guys discussing so seriously today? Is it a continuation of the discussion about freedom?

J: Yes. Freedom, self-knowledge, whether we're more like peaches with a solid seed at the center or more like onions.

M: Assuming we're like peaches, what do you think the pit looks like?

J: It's the "real self" those things that are really in our self-interest. But we've decided that this is something it's quite difficult to know.

M: But you're assuming it's a substantial something?

K: What do you mean?

M: What if it's freedom, self-determination? What if it's not a thing but a quality or a process?

L: Like chocolates with liquid centers?

K: But how does that help us? What we need to find is something that helps tell us how to live, how to act, what has priority, what is an illusion. I think it's got to be something fairly firm. If you're going to choose something and have it be authentically your choice, doesn't there need to be some substantive "you" there to make it?

M: But doesn't freedom imply anything for living, action, choice? Doesn't it imply anything for the way we treat ourselves and others? I think the self may just be freedom.

J: It may, but right now I don't see it. Freedom, all by itself, seems to me to be kind of an empty idea.

L: How do you treat others on the assumption that they can be free and responsible agents? How do you treat yourself? How do you educate children to realize their freedom? Is that what you, May, are asking about when you ask about the implications of freedom?

M: Sure. Good examples.

L: So, going back to our earlier examples of the missionaries and the economists, there is something wrong with replacing one image of self and self-interest if what you put in its place is just another image that isn't supposed to be questioned either. But if you jar loose one image and replace it with the process of self-determination and increased freedom, then that's different?

J: Can you really do that, replace self-identity with freedom?

K: Maybe, but I'm not sure I understand this well enough yet to say if I agree or disagree.

J: Me too. This will take some more thought.

K: And further conversation?

L: For sure. I think this stretches all our thinking.

M: I agree, and it makes me hungry, particularly thinking about peaches, onions, and chocolates with liquid centers.

The Search for the Substantive Self

One of Socrates' principles was that all philosophical knowledge depends on self-knowledge. "Know thyself" operated as a kind of commandment for him and required him to admit openly his own ignorance. Many of Socrates' interlocutors in Plato's dialogues fail to understand some very fundamental philosophical ideas because they fail to know themselves. Self-knowledge was a prerequisite of Socrates' courage as well. How in the world could a man be willing to die for his principles if he did not know, in some very definite sense, that they were more important to him than life itself?

Aristotle made the identification of our human nature essential to the process of discovering the good and happy life. A happy life is a fulfilled life, a life that lives up to its potential, a life that realizes its essential nature. If we do not know what human nature is, Aristotle reasoned, we will not know what a good human life is. Without such knowledge our lives are like a shot in the dark, and we have no knowledge of whether they come close to the target or have missed it completely. Yet we seem to know this. We seem to be able to say, at least in general, that someone has lived a good, full human life and that others have wasted theirs and not lived a fulfilled life. Many people say, for example, that they would rather die than live as a "vegetable" in a permanently comatose state without hope of recovery. How are we able to say this? Apparently because such a life, although still a life, is something less than fully human.

What are the characteristics of a fulfilled human life? Although Aristotle thought that humans will find a great variety of life patterns fulfilling, he believed some things are necessary characteristics of any human life. Here is a paraphrase of his reasoning: A good X (a good anything—apple, cheese sandwich, chisel, dog, pickup truck) is an X that does well what Xs do best. Although we can use a cheese sandwich for many things (a paperweight, a doorstop, a weapon, a mode of communication) we judge the goodness of cheese sandwiches not by how well they do all those things but by how well they do what they do best (i.e., serve as a lunch or snack). A good chisel will be a chisel that does well, not all the things a chisel could imaginably be used to do, but chiseling.

It is this characteristic activity or function that defines the thing and its being a good one of its kind. If the thing being discussed is an organism the characteristic will be more complex, not just an activity, nor a single function, but a form of life.

This characteristic form of life Aristotle called *psyche* or soul. The soul of a wolf is the form of life characteristic of a wolf. The soul of a human is the form of life characteristic of a human. A fully human life is not a static state but is an active form of life characteristic of humans doing what humans do best. If there were a verb form for this activity I suppose it would be called "human-ing." Although humans share many essential activities with other organisms (nutrition, respiration, excretion, reproduction, etc.) these activities do not define the essential human difference, the things that humans do best which makes them fully human. So although such activities are essential, they are not characteristic of the human soul. These characteristic human activities involve the employment of human intellectual gifts in all their variety. We may become a lawyer or a cellist, a writer or a politician, a scientist or a business manager. The important thing is that we live a life that exercises our intellectual capacities. Only then, Aristotle argues, can we be said to have lived a fulfilled human life.

The modern phenomenon of "the couch potato" (i.e., a person who merely eats, excretes, and changes channels), Aristotle would have seen as a tragedy. Here is someone, he would have said, who has assumed that the point of human life is to be passively entertained. Insofar as this person's life is not active, insofar as his or her life does not employ and exercise his or her intellectual capacities, just so far has this person failed to live a complete human life. It is the main function of education, Aristotle thought, to point to the true aim of human life, to model it, and to practice it.

Aristotle, 384–322 B.C.E.

The range of Aristotle's thinking included just about everything that was known or thought about in the Hellenic world. He wrote extensively about biology including a treatise on the behavior of bees, on physics including both terrestrial and celestial motion, on friendship, politics, education, rhetoric, poetry, psychology, ethics, logic, and metaphysics, contributing original and extremely influential thinking in all these areas. In fact, many of these studies owe their initiation to Aristotle. In the field of logic, for example, no one added much to what Aristotle did for over two thousand years. A study of the history of many disciplines begins with reading Aristotle. For covering so many different subjects Aristotle's work is amazingly coherent; what he says about ethics fits well with what he says about biology, what he says about physics fits together well with what he says about logic and psychology. His work remains the model of what a systematic philosophy should be: encyclopedic, coherent, fruitful, and continuingly relevant.

Skepticism About the Substantive Human Self

What reasons do we have to be skeptical of Aristotle's account of essential human nature? We might raise a number of questions:

1. Do humans have enough in common with each other for there to be an essential human nature shared by all? Might there not be a difference—between males and females, for example—sufficient to disallow our finding a common human nature in all of them? Are the differences in humans more basic than the similarities?

2. Is finding an essential human nature basically an inductive process? If we are looking for what all humans share, are we searching for "the lowest common denominator"? If so, the exercise of intellectual capacities doesn't seem to be it. Many people seem (because of birth defects, disease, or accidents) to lack normal adult intellectual capacities. Many others do not find intellectual activities very fulfilling. Does this fact prove Aristotle wrong? If not, why not? If Aristotle is not proceeding inductively to find this common human nature, then how is he proceeding?

3. Is Aristotle's argument shaped by his own prejudices? He is, after all, a very intelligent man, occupied in thinking, theorizing, writing, and

teaching every day. Is it not suspect then, when he comes to the conclusion that the active life of the intellect is the defining characteristic of humanity and the key to a fulfilled human existence? Would he have come to the same conclusion if he had been a peasant farmer or a wife and mother in the average Athenian household? Do theories about what is the essential human nature always reflect prejudices?

4. People in other times and places have come up with different accounts of what the essential human looks like. The ancient Greeks before Aristotle might have said it was to emulate someone like Odysseus—clever, courageous and loyal. The ancient Hebrews might have said it was to emulate someone like Abraham—faithful, patient, and willing to risk all for his God. The stoics would have said it was to be rational in thought and action and in control of one's emotions. Medieval Christians might have said humans were created to contemplate and give glory to God. In the twentieth century Sigmund Freud argued that humans are essentially sexual beings and that everything else we do is largely a manifestation of sex drives. How can we tell which of these versions of human nature is right? Each of them points to certain human characteristics and capacities and makes them paramount. The argument is an interesting and important one, but is there any way to settle it?

5. On the other hand, what do we lose if we stop talking about an essential human nature or stop assuming there is one? When we object to child abuse, on what grounds do we do it? Suppose a parent has hooked his or her young child on drugs? Why would we be upset about this, why regard it as a tragedy? Isn't it because we think that addiction is not a part of a normal, thriving human life? Don't we believe that drug addiction frustrates, rather than enables, a full human life? To suppose this, don't we need to have some kind of working idea about what a full human life is? If so, is total skepticism about this possible? Would denying human nature make such arguments impossible?

Who Am I? The Question of Personal Identity

In some societies the question of who a person is does not often arise. The assumption is that a person is who his or her society sees him or her to be. The objective self, (i.e., the self seen by others), and the subjective self (i.e., the self as seen by oneself) are identical. If I am the chief of a tribal society, my fellow tribal people see me as chief and I understand myself as chief. Chief, if not all of my identity, is at least a large part of it. Such a person, in such a society, will never suffer what we have come to call "an identity crisis." He will never need to take time off to "find himself." Who he is, is a given. Everybody who is part of the society knows it.

As societies become more complex and the idea of the internal self becomes more common, the identity of the objective self and the subjective self is no longer a given. The "discovery" that the inner and outer selves are not identical may be traced very interestingly in the history of ideas. The dramatic tension between what one appears to be and who one is, is a theme in much of literature. Odysseus, in Homer's epic poem, although so well disguised as a beggar that he fools everyone except the family dog, is in fact the king. Jane Austen's heroines, although socially defined in one way, may think of themselves in very different, and often conflicting ways. Contemporary stories about spies, or soap operas about people who suffer from amnesia, are interesting to us because they give us a metaphor for the ambiguous relation between external and internal. Who society supposes we are and who we really are may be quite different.

Jane Austen, 1775–1817

Although Austen's novels were little recognized in her own age, they are much read and studied in our own. Several of them have been made into prizewinning films or serialized for TV (e.g., *Sense and Sensibility, Pride and Prejudice, Persuasion*).

All of Austen's novels examine the concessions and adjustments that a person must make to family duty and social propriety. In particular, they reveal the loneliness and alienation forced on women by social codes and the difficulties that must be faced by women who challenge them. Even though most of her novels come to a "happy ending" with the marriage of the principal characters, the reader is made to realize what such happiness costs. So rather than caving in to the conventions of the day, Austen tells romantic stories with a sense of tragedy and irony.

Some people in the contemporary world assume that everyone has an identity, a fate, as it were, that is given to them. If they can only discover it and orient themselves to it, the assumption goes, then a happy and fulfilled life will follow. This is the premise that stands behind the making and reading of horoscopes, for example. I remember a radio advertisement for an astrologer that closed with the line, "If you know your stars you'll know who you are. If you know who you are you'll know what to do. Call today for your reading and get your life on the road to happiness."

There are two directions that skepticism can go from such claims about the essential self. (1) We may believe that everyone has a self whom they really are, but doubt whether there's any privileged way to find out what this self is. This seems to be the view of most college students. They explore different fields of study, different friends, different relationships, different jobs, until they find one that "fits." Apart from trying out different life courses they don't know how to tell what's right for them, hence the experimental approach is the one they resort to. But the "fit" of a life choice is also hard to judge as is witnessed by the proportion of marriages that end in divorce and the large number of people who return to the university in midcareer in order to pursue another direction. I have met bank vice presidents, symphony violinists, accountants, owners of businesses, attorneys, teachers, nurses, all of whom were very successful in their professions, beginning again at thirty-five, forty, sometimes even at fifty, to look for a new life orientation. (2) We may doubt that there is any such thing as the essential self at all. All searching for who one is, all fuss about identity, all looking for something that fits the self I am, is a mistake from this point of view. In what follows we review four arguments against the idea that there is an essential self. All are skeptical, but for surprisingly different reasons.

Nietzsche's Argument

Friedrich Nietzsche argued that the ideas of God and the self occur to us because they are grammatical mistakes, that is, incorrect inferences from grammar to reality. While the idea of the self as source of our actions, as will, or as the subject that thinks or acts comes up again and again in our language (I want, I intend, I doubt, I do) Nietzsche claims that we ought not, as Descartes had done, infer the existence of a self from this grammatical feature. Nietzsche stated,

> [O]wing to the seduction of language (and of the fundamental errors of reason that are petrified in it) all effects are misconceived as conditioned by something that causes effects, by a "subject,"
> . . . For just as the popular mind separates the lightning from its flash and takes the latter for an action, . . . so popular morality also separates strength from expressions of strength, as if there were a neutral substratum behind the strong man, which was free to express strength or not to do so. But there is no such substratum; there is no "being" behind the doing, effecting, becoming; "the doer" is simply a fiction added to the deed—the deed is

everything. . . . No wonder if the submerged, darkly glowering emotions of vengefulness and hatred exploit this belief for their own ends and in fact maintain no belief more ardently than that the strong man is free to be weak and the bird of prey to be a lamb—for thus they gain the right to make the bird of prey accountable for being a bird of prey. (*Genealogy of Morals*, I, 13)

Morality and the law both depend on the idea that someone can be blamed and praised for action. In order to make sense of punishing a person for a murder he or she committed years ago, we need to maintain that he or she is substantially the same person. "*You* must be punished for what *you* did." This statement only makes sense if there is some kind of identity between the two 'you's.' Of course this is not an argument that would have convinced Nietzsche, for he was just as critical of morality and the institutions that supported it as he was of the idea of the substantial self. We believe in such a self, he argued, because we desire to blame and punish. We justify the belief by arguing from a feature of our grammar (the subject in the sentence) to a feature of reality (the self behind the action).

Some Buddhist and Christian Views of the Self

Although I doubt anything is *the* Christian view of the self, many Christian thinkers maintain that the self, or at least the egoistic, selfish self, is the source of all human evil, and that selfishness and sin are, in fact, the same. Interestingly this is also a view common among Buddhist thinkers. Buddhists are more likely to say the selfish self is an illusion, but one that lies at the heart of all human suffering. The annihilation of this self, this controlling illusion, is a necessary step on the way to enlightenment. Christian thinkers are more likely to use the metaphor of death of the self, borrowing the language of Christ's crucifixion. As St. Paul wrote, "I die with Christ to be raised again in him" (Romans 6:3). Describing this resurrected self, he stated, "It is no longer I who live but Christ who lives in me" (Galatians 2:20).

At the same time that both Christianity and Buddhism assert the necessity of losing the egocentric self, both also contain teachings that reinforce the idea of a continuing personal identity. What sense does the Buddhist idea of reincarnation make if there is no essential identity between the incarnations? What sense is there to the Christian idea of a resurrected life if there is nothing to connect the new life to the old one? What sense does the "re" part of both of those words make if there is no continuity of identity? So this leaves us with a problem in attempting to talk about Buddhist and Christian views of the self. Which of these models are we supposed to follow: that the self is a problem or illusion to be overcome or that it is a necessary feature of Christian and Buddhist understanding?

Sartre's Argument

Jean-Paul Sartre's (1905–1980) argument has some things in common with Nietzsche's view, but attacks the problem from a slightly different angle. The self is not, Sartre argues, a thing. It is consciousness, not a thing that is conscious like the "thinking thing" of Descartes, but consciousness itself. Consciousness, unlike the things that are the objects of consciousness, is insubstantial. Compared to the givenness and solidity of objects, it is literally *nothing*. The nothing that consciousness is, Sartre argues, is what gives us freedom, the ability to negate anything that is given. Sartre writes,

> Man is free because he is not himself but presence to himself. The being which is what it is cannot be free. Freedom is precisely the nothingness which is made-to-be at the heart of man and which forces human reality to make itself instead of to be. . . . for human reality, to be is to choose oneself. . . . (*Being & Nothingness*, IV, 1, 538)

Thus we have an identity, an established self, only in the past tense. I can talk about what I have done and who I have been. This past self is an object, a given; it has a describable nature that is equivalent to my past history. But I am not equal to my past. I can use my past in many ways: affirm it, deny it, rebel against it, use parts of it, forget it. But what I make of my own past I do in my own freedom (i.e., I am not "fated" to continue my past into my future). I can, if I wish, become someone quite different than I have ever been. My self, in other words, is constantly being created in every present moment. "My existence," as Sartre puts it, "precedes my essence." Until I am dead, no one can finally describe who I am. What I do tomorrow may prove them completely mistaken.

Sartre objects to the substantial self because he wants to affirm a radical freedom. The only essence or nature we have as humans is *no essence* (i.e., our freedom to be whomever we choose). The self is continually recreated in freedom. Sartre points out that not everyone is willing to accept this amount of freedom. Radical freedom makes us realize that we cannot trust even ourselves. Someone might say, "I trust old Joe. Why, I know him as well as I know my own self." But what happens if neither Joe nor my own self is something that can really be known? Can I bear living with a stranger? Sartre expresses the anxiety of such a life in the metaphor of condemnation: "I am condemned to exist forever beyond my essence, beyond the causes and motives of my act. I am condemned to be free" (537).

Jean Anouilh, 1910–1987

Anouilh, noted French playwright, is probably the most philosophical dramatist of the twentieth century. His plays explore classical questions about the human condition that arise acutely in the contemporary world. Anouilh has taken the themes of Greek tragedy (e.g., *Eurydice*, 1941, and *Antigone*, 1944) and set them in the context of twentieth-century calamities (e.g., World War II). Even his comedies and lighter pieces (e.g., *The Waltz of the Toreadors*, 1952) have a fierceness to them because of the issues they focus on and the questions they raise. Anouilh's plays work very well as a stimulus to discussion as well as illustrations of the kinds of issues philosophers raise.

Jean Anouihl, in his play *Traveler Without Luggage*, tells the story of a man who awakens one morning with no memory of who he is. He goes through his pockets, luggage, things he might have brought with him, looking for some clue as to who he is. But he finds nothing. Is he a murderer? A spy? If so, for whom? Is he rich or poor? Is he greedy and ruthless or is he a pious, gentle man? He doesn't know, and not knowing frightens him. Sartre would say we are all exactly like this man except that although we may know who we have been, we still do not know who we are.

Sartre says that we use all kinds of devices to avoid realizing our own freedom. We may pretend that our social role *is* our identity. Our job, then, not only is something that we do, but someone who we are. Or we may place the blame for our actions on our nature, rather than accepting responsibility for them as our own free actions. Consider the following imaginary dialogue as illustrating this latter point:

Teacher: You've missed many classes in a row, Jerome, including the test we had last Thursday. What seems to be the problem?

Jerome: I overslept.

T: You overslept for a 10:30 class? And so many times in a row? A person might oversleep once, but then you solve the problem! This looks more like a very bad habit.

J: Yeah, I know. I don't know why I do that. I guess I'm just basically a lazy person.

T: Well, change your behavior quickly or you're going to flunk this class!

J: But how can I change, if that's the way I am?

T: Laziness is what you do, it's not who you are, for goodness sake. Just decide you want to change this pattern and do it.

J: I'm not sure I can. As I said, that's just the way I am.

T: Nonsense! That's nothing but an excuse. Take responsibility for your life! I expect you to have this work made up in one week. Now get to it!

Simone de Beauvoir (1908–1986) intellectual colleague and long-time friend of Sartre, basically agreed with his account of human freedom (e.g., in her book *The Ethics of Ambiguity*). But she also suggested that human freedom is bound by the conditions of our lives that we do not personally create (e.g., our gender). In her groundbreaking book *The Second Sex*, she suggests that being female presents a unique set of difficulties to the realization of freedom. The identity of woman, she points out, is partially fixed because she is defined by men as "the second sex." Man, therefore, is the standard of what it means to be human, woman thus is "the other." So woman does not get to choose her self because an identity (as well as a kind of alienation) has been chosen for her. She writes,

> What is a woman? . . . Is this attribute something secreted by the ovaries? Or is it a Platonic essence, a product of the philosophic imagination? Is a rustling petticoat enough to bring it down to earth? Although some women try zealously to embody this essence it is hardly patentable. . . . To state the question is, to me, to suggest a preliminary answer. The fact that I need ask it is itself significant. A man would never get the idea of writing a book on the peculiar situation of the human male. . . . for man represents both the positive and the neutral . . . whereas woman represents the negative . . . a lack . . . an imperfect being. (Introduction)

Dostoevsky's Underground Man

Fyodor Dostoevsky, in his short novel *Notes from Underground*, creates a complex character who shares the twists and turns of his own thought. This character is extremely reflective and is very good at examining his own motives for action. He has made self-criticism into a fine art. Whenever he is about to do or say anything, he is already there criticizing his (as well as other people's) reasons for doing it or saying it.

I am a sick man . . . I am a spiteful man. I am an unpleasant man. I think my liver is diseased. However I don't know beans about my disease, and I am not sure what is bothering me. I don't treat it and I never have, though I respect medicine and doctors. . . . No, I refuse to treat it out of spite. You probably will not understand that. Well, but I understand it.

Fyodor Dostoevsky, 1821–1881

Dostoevsky is one of the world's truly great novelists. Long before psychology existed as a discipline Dostoevsky's novels achieved astounding depth of understanding into the complexities and failures of the human psyche. His famous work *Crime and Punishment* examines the psychology of a young man who commits robbery and murder. He finally comes to realize the full calamity of his deed. Nietzsche paid a rare but somewhat characteristic compliment when he said, "Dostoevsky is the only psychologist from whom I have anything to learn."

Dostoevsky's novels mirror many of the events in his life. He was imprisoned for several years in Siberia (*The House of the Dead*) and was nearly killed by firing squad but pardoned at the last moment (*The Idiot*). He was also addicted to gambling (*The Gambler*) and spent much of his life living in extreme poverty.

To a greater degree than any of his predecessors, Dostoevsky developed novels in which strong characters are set off against each other. Rather than novels that have a main protagonist surrounded by several lesser ones, Dostoevsky created novels (e.g., *The Brothers Karamazov*) in which very different characters and temperaments are set off in dialogue with each other. None of them dominates, and the tension of the novel arises from the unresolved conflict between them. The reader is led to wonder on which side of these disputes the author would have argued, all of them are so convincingly stated. Dostoevsky's texts are often excerpted in philosophy anthologies in discussions of human nature and the nature of evil, because they raise these philosophical issues so graphically.

I have been living like this for twenty years now. I am forty. I used to be in the civil service, but no longer am. I was a spiteful official. I was rude and took pleasure in being so. After all, I did not accept bribes, so I was bound to find compensation in that, at least. (A bad joke but I will not cross it out, I wrote it thinking it would sound witty; but now that I see myself that I only wanted to show off in a despicable way, I will purposely not cross it out!) . . .

I was lying just now when I said I was a spiteful official. I was lying out of spite. . . . Not only could I not become spiteful, I could not become anything: neither spiteful nor kind, neither a rascal nor an honest man, neither a hero nor an insect. Now I am living out my life in my corner, taunting myself with the spiteful and useless consolation that an intelligent man cannot seriously become anything and that only a fool can become something. Yes, an intelligent man in the nineteenth century must and morally ought to be preeminently a characterless creature; a man of character, an active man, is preeminently a limited creature. . . .

Now I want to tell you . . . why I could not even become an insect. I tell you solemnly that I wanted to become an insect many times. But I was not even worthy of that. . . . to be hyper-conscious is a disease, a real positive disease. . . . I am firmly convinced not only that a great deal of consciousness, but that any consciousness, is a disease.

After all, people who know how to revenge themselves and take care of themselves in general, how do they do it? . . . when they are possessed, let us suppose, by a feeling of revenge, then for the time there is nothing else but that feeling left in their whole being. Such a man simply rushes straight for his object like an infuriated bull. . . . Well, such a direct person I regard as the normal man. . . . Such a man I envy till I am green in the face. He is stupid, . . . but perhaps the normal man should be stupid. . . . The antithesis of the normal man [is] . . . the hyper-conscious man.

All straightforward persons and men of action are active because they are stupid and limited. How can that be explained? . . . as a result of their limitation they take immediate and secondary causes for primary ones, and in that persuade themselves more quickly and easily . . . that they have found an infallible basis for their activity, and their minds are at ease. . . . To begin to act, you know, you must first have your mind completely at ease and without a trace of doubt in it. Well, how am I, for example, to set my mind at ease? Where are the primary causes on which I am to build? . . . I, and every person of intelligence, can see through them completely. (*Notes from Underground*, 3-5)

A Web of Questions

What is this character's problem? Does he lack freedom? Or does he have so much freedom that he is paralyzed by it? Is he, as he claims, too self-conscious? Or is it possible that there is some consciousness he lacks? Does this man know himself too well? Or is it his problem that he is unable to know himself? Is it possible that both alternatives are true? If this is so, what do we learn about freedom from this example?

What are the conditions for freedom? Must the self, as Sartre suggests, really be a "nothing" before freedom is possible? Or is it the case that a self which is "nothing" cannot choose at all, as Dostoevsky's character suggests? Is a choice based on nothing any different than simply flipping a coin? In what sense, then, is this a *choice* at all? If we made all our decisions by confronting a menu of choices and rolling a die with the appropriate number of sides, would that constitute freedom? If I am to create my self and be responsible for the self I create, can I create such a self out of nothing? Or must there already be a substantial self who is the creator? How in the world do we enable creative freedom?

Are the most creative people persons with a clear identity or without one? When Picasso confronted a fresh blank canvas he certainly did not want to paint the same picture he painted the day before. But the painting that Picasso makes on a given day will have something in common, stylistically, thematically, structurally, historically, with the other work he has done before. We can tell a Picasso when we see one—so there must be some part of his identity in the way he paints. Picasso was an extraordinarily creative artist, but not because he every day became a totally different artist. There is continuity in his creative development, and room for creativity within the continuity.

Questions for Further Reflection

1. In the opening dialogue, the argument swings between two points of view—that freedom requires we know who we are, and that freedom occurs only when there is no self to be known. Which, if either, of these alternatives makes the most sense to you? Fully explain your reasons.

2. The earlier discussion of Socrates (p. 91, ff.) suggests that courage requires self-knowledge. Do you agree? Can you think of any exceptions to this? Did reading the passage from Dostoevsky change your mind about this? Does bold action require self-knowledge—or self-ignorance?

3. What advantages are there in arguing that we all share a basic human nature? For what reasons might we want to be skeptical of such claims?

4. What would you say are the characteristics of a fulfilled human life? Make a list of the characteristics you admire in others, the characteristics you'd like to see developed in yourself, or that you'd like to see developed in your own children. How is your model of the fulfilled human like or unlike Aristotle's? What are the influences that have helped shape your views on this issue?

5. How would you respond to Nietzsche's claim that the self is an attempt on the part of the weak to make the strong feel guilty for their strength? If you accept Nietzsche's argument, what other ideas besides the self may function in a similar way?

6. In what ways is a free person analogous to Anouilh's amnesiac (p. 99, ff.)? Are there any ways in which freedom is more analogous to finally remembering who one is?

7. De Beauvoir suggests that being female presents a different set of problems for identity and freedom than those faced by a male. Do you agree with this assessment? If so, what, specifically are they? If you disagree, what are your reasons?

8. Dostoevsky's "underground man" concludes that a "man of action" cannot be reflective, but must, in fact, be stupid. Can you think of real-life examples that verify this? Can you think of counterexamples?

9. Does the Christian and Buddhist view that the self must die or be annihilated make sense to you? How do you understand their claims that a new Christ-self or Buddha-self can replace the old one? How does this transformation take place and what is it like?

10. Suppose you wanted your children to grow up to be free and creative persons. How would you help and enable them to do this? What styles of parenting and or education are consistent and inconsistent with such a goal?

Works Cited

de Beauvoir, Simone. *The Ethics of Ambiguity*, trans. B. Frechtman. Secaucus, N.J.: Citadel Press, 1950.

———. *The Second Sex*, trans. by H.M. Parshley. New York: Alfred A. Knopf, 1962.

Dostoevsky, Fyodor. *Notes from Underground*, trans. R. Matlaw. New York: Dutton, 1960.

Nietzsche, Friedrich. *The Genealogy of Morals*, trans. F. Golffing. Garden City, N.Y.: Doubleday, 1956.

Sartre, Jean Paul. *Being and Nothingness*, trans. H. Barnes. New York: Philosophical Library, 1956.

St. Paul. Epistle to the Romans, Epistle to the Galatians, *New English Bible*. Oxford: Oxford University Press, 1984.

CHAPTER EIGHT

Questions, Questions, and More Questions!

Anyone reading this book will have already realized that philosophers pose a lot of questions. Is that a failure of philosophy—or one of its strengths? This chapter offers six answers to these two questions.

Dialogue VIII

Niara: You know, I find philosophy very interesting, but I also find it very frustrating.

Otis: Yeah, I know what you mean. Philosophers are constantly opening new inquiries but they never seem to get any answers, at least not answers that everybody is happy with. Philosophy doesn't seem to make any progress.

N: I wouldn't go so far as to say that. In the process of discussion you find out a lot of answers that just won't work, that are over-simplifications or that look at only part of the issue. That's a kind of progress.

O: Yeah, I guess. But it's like progress from simpleminded confusion to a complex, sophisticated confusion. I'd like to see the kind of progress people have made in chemistry or physics, where we really know a lot more now than people used to. In philosophy we keep going back to the beginning. In physics we never study the works of ancient physicists. They just didn't know very much. But in philosophy it's some of those ancient guys who seem to be the wisest. That's kind of odd, isn't it?

N: Not really. You have to realize that we read those ancient philosophers a lot differently than they were read by their contemporaries. We've seen some directions that things have gone and we know where the dangers and dead ends lie, so we don't have to go down those roads again. That's what makes it profitable for each age to study those ancient writers over again. We see things in a different way. A postmodern reading of Plato is going to see different things there than an Enlightenment reading of Plato would have seen. The works of ancient physics probably just aren't as relevant or interesting, just wrong.

O: Just the same, wouldn't it be nice if philosophy produced some real knowledge?

N: I think it does.

O: Like what?

N: Heck, I can think of quite a few important philosophical truths right off the top of my head: (1) It's a mistake to give an objective account of things and leave out what the thinking subject contributes to it. (2) Language shapes our concepts and concepts shape our thinking. We can't escape from our language embededness. (3) Language, in turn, is shaped by the culture, the institutions, the intellectual dialogue that takes place in a society and between societies. (4) Just because our language has a name for something doesn't mean there's a reality there that corresponds to that name. Language can both represent and misrepresent reality.

O: OK, that's an impressive start. I wonder how many more such things we could come up with if we tried? But if there are such "truths" discovered by philosophy, and I think that you're right that there are, why doesn't someone write a standard textbook that lists them, the way freshman-level textbooks do in other studies?

N: Good question. But we have to realize that other disciplines have their continuing disputes the same way philosophy does, it's just that other disciplines don't put these disputes out front the way philosophers do. In an introductory physics class you learn all the stuff physicists agree about. In an introductory philosophy class you'll mainly learn the things philosophers disagree about. Why do you think that is?

O: In physics you get to controversial issues only when you're a grad student. In philosophy you get to them right away. But a lot of the early study in the sciences is like learning a foreign language. First you learn the language, then later you actually get to be an inquirer in it. Philosophers, for the most part, use ordinary language; that's why the inquiry can begin earlier.

N: You're right. That's an interesting comparison. I hadn't thought of it like that before. Might it also be that in philosophy the answers aren't always as important as the asking of questions? An engineer can use the answer a physicist comes up with, without doing the inquiry herself. In philosophy the answers aren't worth much to people who haven't done the inquiry.

O: You're right. The things that interest me most about philosophy are those things I'm able to appropriate personally. Merely reading a list of someone else's discoveries doesn't make them discoveries for me. In philosophy that's important.

N: So have you satisfied your original frustration with philosophy? I think I have.

O: In a way. But also in a way not. It's just that now I'm not as bothered about it. I think a continuing frustration may be appropriate to philosophers. Lots of philosophers have wished their discipline was more like something else, mathematics, physics, and so on.

N: True. But we must remember that the effort to remodel philosophy to be more like math or science has almost always resulted in doing philosophy badly.

O: You mean you think someone like Descartes was a bad philosopher? He certainly is one of the most important philosophers to study.

N: Yes, but that's because he made such significant and far-reaching mistakes. He's important to study as a bad example.

O: Hold it! I thoroughly disagree. But I can see this is the topic for a whole new debate. How about Wednesday at lunch?

N: OK, I'm available!

Why Do Philosophers Respond to Questions with More Questions?

Sometimes even when philosophers answer questions, the answers end up generating more questions or questions of a different order. This happened with the web of questions that ended Chapter Seven. This also will happen in this chapter. We will look at a number of possible answers to this opening question. But at the end we will still be left with another question: Which, if any, of these answers is the best one?

Answer 1. Philosophy is question focused because it attracts people to it who, like attorneys, are argumentative and disputatious. Neither philosophy nor the law tend to attract mediators or compromisers. Both philosophers and attorneys focus on points of disagreement and take exception to what others say. The sciences, in contrast, attract people who are willing to work together on research teams, willing to follow instructions, more willing to fall in line because that's the way things get done. If philosophy were organized differently as an inquiry so that people worked together on research teams, there would be more answers at the end and not so many unanswered questions. As it stands, most of the work that philosophers do, at least what is published in philosophical journals, is to criticize each other.

David Hume, 1711–1776
and Immanuel Kant, 1724–1804

The careers of Hume and Kant span the eighteenth century, a period often called the Age of Enlightenment. It was a period when many philosophers argued for the powers of human reason to overcome the Age of Belief that had preceded and expected reason to solve all human problems. It was also an age of revolution. Both in France and the United States, thinkers were arguing that government ruled not by "divine right" but only by the "the consent of the governed." On the basis of such ideas British colonial rule was overthrown in America and the king and queen of France were deposed and finally beheaded.

Hume and Kant are, in some respects, typical of Enlightenment thinkers. Both, for example, argue that morality is based on human experience and reason, not on divine authority or tradition. In other respects, however, Hume and Kant are atypical. Both, for example, argued that human powers of knowing are severely limited to things that fall within our range of experience. Beyond the range of experience we may be tempted to speculate, but we must admit that we have no ability to claim to *know* anything.

Hume closes his famous book, *An Enquiry Concerning Human Understanding*, with these words: "When we run over libraries persuaded of these principles [the limits of human knowledge], what havoc must we make? If we take in our hand any volume of divinity or school metaphysics, for instance, let us ask, Does it contain any abstract reasoning concerning quantity or number? No. Does it contain any experimental reasoning concerning matter of fact and existence? No. Commit it then to the flames; for it can contain nothing but sophistry and illusion."

Answer 2. Philosophical answers always generate more questions because there is something wrong with the initial questions. What is wrong? Let us look at a few possibilities. The questions may go beyond any human's ability to answer them. This is what David Hume and Immanuel Kant believed was the problem with metaphysical questions; they were questions that would require, to be answered adequately, data that simply go beyond human experience. We can perfectly well answer questions about how much time some process takes because the process can be experienced and measured. But we cannot answer questions about time itself because time is not an object of experience. We should learn to distinguish between questions that can be empirically answered and those that cannot. And about the latter, presumably, we should keep quiet. Interestingly, neither Hume nor Kant was completely happy with that conclusion, and Kant was anything but quiet about things beyond human experience.

Another reading of the problem with philosophical questions is given by Ludwig Wittgenstein. He argued that philosophical questions ought not be answered because the questions themselves lead us off in directions that we ought not follow. So Wittgenstein found fault with many philosophical questions, and thought that we ought to question theories that purport to answer them. Wittgenstein pointed to the harm done by questions that oversimplify, questions like "How does language signify?" The problem with such a question is that it tempts us to look for *the* way that language signifies, or has meaning. Such a question is likely to spawn various accounts which purport to be *the theory* of linguistic meaning. The problem is that language does not signify in one way, but in many, many very different ways. Wittgenstein used the following analogy:

> 11. [W]hat confuses us is the uniform appearance of words when we hear them spoken or meet them in script and print. For their application is not presented to us so clearly. Especially when we are doing philosophy!

> 12. It is like looking into the cabin of a locomotive. We see handles looking more or less alike. (Naturally since they are all supposed to be handled.) But one is the handle of a crank which can be moved continuously . . . another is the handle of a switch, which has only two effective positions, it is either off or on; a third is the handle of a brake-lever, the harder one pulls on it the harder it brakes; the fourth the handle of a pump: it has an effect only so long as it is moved to and fro.

Ludwig Wittgenstein, 1889–1951

Austrian born, Wittgenstein spent most of his academic career at Cambridge University in England. His first book, usually known as the *Tractatus*, consisted of terse, often enigmatic propositions numbered so as to show their logical relation to each other. For example, the book opens:

> 1.   *The world is all that is the case.*
> 1.1   *The world is the totality of facts, not of things.*
> 1.11 *The world is determined by the facts, and by their being all the facts.*
> 1.12 *For the totality of facts determines what is the case, and also whatever is not the case.*
> 1.13 *The facts in logical space are the world, etc.*

and ends:

> 6.54 *My propositions serve as elucidations in the following way: anyone who understands me eventually recognizes them as nonsensical, when he has used them—as steps—to climb up beyond them. (He must, so to speak, throw away the ladder after he has climbed up it.) He must transcend these propositions, and then he will see the world aright.*

7.   *What we cannot speak about we must consign to silence.*

Later in his life Wittgenstein both changed his mind about many of the things he wrote in the *Tractatus* and also changed quite drastically his style of writing philosophy. His *Philosophical Investigations* is a series of reflections, almost internal dialogues, about the ways we understand and misunderstand the language we use to think in. For example:

335.   *What happens when we make an effort—say in writing a letter—to find the right expression for our thoughts? . . . Now if it were asked: "Do you have the thought before finding the expression?" what would one have to reply? And what, to the question: "What did the thought consist in, as it existed before the expression?"*

Wittgenstein is not only a challenging thinker but is also one of the fascinating characters in twentieth-century philosophy. At an early age he rejected a large inheritance, lived in extreme simplicity, served as an elementary school teacher, and for a time, lived a hermit's life in a hut on the coast of Norway. He also made efforts to persuade his students not to become professional philosophers but to pursue more practical careers. Most did not take his advice.

Answer 3. Philosophical questions are not finitely answerable, but that is not a fault of the questions but a fault in the nature of answers. Let us employ an analogy introduced by Socrates in Plato's dialogue *Meno*. Socrates asks a slave boy to help him solve a problem in geometry: what is the length of a side of a square that has twice the area of 4 square units? Put into modern language, the question is, what is the square root of 8? The slave boy sees that a square of 4 square units has a side 2 units long. Because he's looking for the side of a square twice as big, he suggests the answer is twice 2, or 4 units long. Clearly, this is incorrect, for a side of 4 units produces a square of 16 units, twice too big. Because 4 is twice too big and 2 is twice too small, the slave boy reasons that if he splits the difference he will get the right answer. So he suggests a side of 3. But a side of 3 produces a square of 9, not 8. Three is too big so he guesses 2 1/2, which is too small. What the boy does not come to realize is that any answer he gives will not be precisely right. Every finite answer is either too big or too small. The correct answer would require an infinite number of qualifications to be correct; consequently one would never reach it by this method of approximation.

Although Socrates may leave the slave (or any interlocutor) frustrated at his inability to say the correct answer, Socrates at the same time shows that the answer is plainly in view. The length we are looking for is, of course, the diagonal of the original square of 4. Here we have an answer that we can be led to see; an answer *that can be shown*—but it is an answer *that cannot be said,* at least not in a finite way.

Is this also the problem with philosophy? If so, the difficulty does not lie with the scope or the direction of the questions asked, but with the smallness of our understanding of what an answer is. If there are answers that can be shown, that can somehow be pointed toward, but cannot precisely be said, then philosophy may produce a kind of knowledge after all, just not the sort we may have been expecting. The problem lies, then, not with the answers but with our expectations.

Answer 4. Philosophy produces more questions than answers because reality is by its very nature ambiguous. Reality, according to this theory, is like the elephant encountered by the blind men. It not only combines the features of a wall, a snake, a tree, a spear, a palm leaf, a rope, and so on, but combines them in ways that positively invite different and competing interpretations. Some texts, I think of Shakespeare's *Hamlet* and Mary Shelley's *Frankenstein* as examples, invite alternative and even opposing interpretations. Perhaps reality is like this as well. If so, it would explain why a philosophical theory or answer always invites more questions. If ambiguity lies not only in the practice of interpretation but in the reality to be interpreted itself, the unfinished nature of philosophical answers is the only appropriate response. To pretend to have given *the account* of reality, like the pretense of giving *the account* of Hamlet, is where the problem lies. To end with questions is the only appropriate way to end if the text or the reality one interprets is, in fact, ambiguous.

Answer 5. Philosophy, rightly done, always ends with questions because it deals with things that are more adequately described as mystery than as problems. Gabriel Marcel (1889–1973) distinguishes between a problem and a mystery as follows:

> A problem is something I meet, which I find complete before me, which I can therefore lay siege to and reduce. All problems may, in principle, yield verifiable solutions. (*Being & Having,* 117) A mystery is meta-problematic . . . it is a problem which encroaches upon its own data, invading them, as it were, and thereby transcending them as a simple problem. . . . In reflecting on a mystery

we tend inevitably to degrade it to the level of a problem. ("On the Ontological Mystery," 19)

Marcel gives several examples of things which are mysteries that we try to reduce to problems: the union of body and soul, the nature of evil, love and human relationship, self identity, freedom, the nature of being, being with others. It is not possible to do justice to such things in an objective, detached way and solve them as problems, for each includes the stance of the person thinking about it as part of the issue. Like a closed loop, thinking about evil or love or freedom takes us back to the lived response of the thinker. We think most adequately about such a subject when we don't fall for the temptation of oversimplifying it. The deep complexity of the questions and the passionate involvement of the questioner may more adequately express the issue than an oversimplified answer could. Marcel states,

> In such a world [a world reduced to problems] the ontological need, the need of being, is exhausted in exact proportion to the breaking down of personality on the one hand and, on the other, to the triumph of the category of the "purely natural" and the consequent atrophy of the faculty of wonder. ("On the Ontological Mystery," 13)

So if philosophical inquiries are about mystery instead of just about problems, they ought to resist being answerable. The lack of finality in the inquiry, rather than being a sign of failure, would then be a sign that the depth and recursiveness of the issue has been respected. Answers suggest that we, as inquirers, have finally arrived at the end of our journey. Marcel would say that we have not arrived and never will. We are, as human beings, continually "on the way."

Iris Murdoch seems to have a similar view of philosophy, although she does not use Marcel's language of "mystery" to describe it. Instead she sees it as the peculiar role of philosophy to return again and again to the beginnings, to question again what seemed so obvious to the generation before. She writes,

> It is sometimes said, either irritably or with a certain satisfaction, that philosophy makes no progress. It is certainly true, and I think this is an abiding and not a regrettable characteristic of the discipline, that philosophy has in a sense to keep trying to return to the beginning: a thing which is not at all easy to do. There is a two-way movement in philosophy, a movement towards the building of elaborate theories, and a move back again towards the consideration of simple but obvious facts. McTaggart says that

time is unreal, Moore replies that he has just had his breakfast. Both these aspects of philosophy are necessary to it. ("The Idea of Perfection," 1)

Murdoch's point is that for philosophy to end with a question is not a sign of philosophy's failure, but a sign of its success. The question at the end indicates that the philosopher is willing once again to compare theory to reality.

Answer 6. Most people (and most disciplines) overvalue answers and devalue questions; philosophy does (and ought to do) the opposite. In Chapter Two we noted that something can be a correct answer and yet function more as a name for our ignorance than as something that actually advances our understanding. Gravity was one example we used then. Consider the following dialogue:

Students: We've heard that you believe in UFOs? Is this true?

Teacher: Yes, I certainly do.

S: But you seem like a rational person. Why do you believe in something like that?

T: The best reason a person could have—because I've seen them.

S: Really? You've seen UFOs?

T: Sure, hasn't everybody?

S: No way. We've never seen them.

T: Do you really mean to tell me you've never seen something in the sky that you couldn't identify? You've never seen anything that you didn't know what it was?

S: Oh sure. But—

T: Well, isn't that what UFO means? A flying object that one has not identified?

S: Well, we meant flying saucers, spaceships from alien planets, stuff like that.

T: But that isn't what UFO means. Unidentified flying object—it means we don't know what in the world it is. Right?

S: Yeah, I guess that's what it means, but then the claim to have seen one is not anywhere near so interesting.

T: Yes, well, I never claimed that it was.

The claim to have seen alien spaceships is indeed a good deal more interesting than the claim to have seen something one didn't understand. But how quick we are to take a word that means "I don't understand it" and translate it into a claim of the wildest sort.

It is also sometimes possible to make ourselves believe that the question, restated, is really its own answer. When I use the example mentioned earlier in this chapter, "What is the side of a square with the area of 8?" students usually quickly respond with the "answer." "It's the square root of 8." I usually respond to them that this is not an answer, but simply the question restated. It is as though we answered the question "What is the side of a square with the area 8?" by saying "It is the side of a square with the area 8." This may serve as a kind of an answer, even the correct one in some contexts, but it's important to notice that we know nothing more by knowing such an answer than we knew when we only knew the question.

Together with the temptation to overvalue answers also comes the temptation to devalue questions. Questions, particularly well-thought-out questions, are not nothing. Very often they indicate the nature and quality of a person's thinking better than her answers do. Rather than having students turn in summaries of their readings for a class, I will frequently ask them to turn in a list of questions that occurred to them while reading. I can usually tell more about their understanding of the text and about the level of their engagement with it from their questions than from their summaries.

Questions are not innocent. My nine-year-old son a few weeks ago asked me, "Is a mushroom a vegetable?" I responded, "No, not really." He then asked, "Well then, what *food group* does it belong to?" His initial question had an agenda of categories embedded in it. If I had asked, "Vegetable, as opposed to what?" I might have understood what he was asking much better and consequently have answered better. His response was to say, "I think they're most like meat, because you often find them in gravy and on pizza."

Questions have the power to perform many positive functions. They direct our attention, telling us where, and at what level to look. They initiate, enable, and stimulate inquiry. They have the ability to uncover, reveal, and open us to new dimensions of experience. Along with this power also comes the power to mislead, misdirect attention, and to bring along limiting and reductive agendas. A lot of assumptions can be built into a question, assumptions about focus, method, and the categories for available answers. To end with a mess of questions may be a very significant ending, provided that the questions do what excellent questions can do. Finally, questions are usually a more adequate expression of wonder than answers are. If wonder is, as Plato said, the governing principle of philosophy, then philosophy may do well to end with excellent questions and not worry about not having many answers.

Questions for Further Reflection

1. In the dialogue (p.108) Niara cites four things that she considers examples of philosophical discoveries. Can you add to the list? How does this list differ from the kinds of discoveries one might make in physics? In sociology or psychology? In history or anthropology?

2. The dialogue suggests there might be a textbook of "philosophical answers" to be used in introductory courses. What do you think about this idea? How would this change the learning and teaching of philosophy? What kinds of things might such a text include?

3. Hume and Kant, among others, fault philosophical questions and theories that go beyond experience. Where are the limits of experience? What kinds of questions would be out of bounds if we took Hume and Kant as guides?

4. Answer 3 suggests there are some philosophical truths that can be shown and seen but cannot strictly be said. Can you give an example? If this is the case, what does it suggest about the appropriate method of teaching and learning in philosophy?

5. Give an example where the reality being interpreted is ambiguous. Does the discovery of such basic ambiguity occur in other disciplines than in philosophy? Give examples. In such cases is the best kind of theory an eclectic theory (i.e., one that, like a patchwork quilt, combines aspects of all theories)?

6. Can you think of a term or idea which, like *UFO,* began by being a confession of ignorance but has evolved into an idea that people generally think they understand? Does the term *mystery* employed by Marcel work in this way? Why or why not?

7. At several points in this chapter I suggest it is important to differentiate between good philosophical questions and misleading ones. What general characteristics should we look for in questions to allow us to tell the difference?

8. Which of the six answers given in this chapter is the best? Give your reasons as well as the criteria you used in choosing. Which answer would you say is worst? Why? Do you see the questions at the end of the inquiry as a sign of failure or as a sign of success?

9. Consider again what H.L. Mencken wrote: "For every complex question there is a simple answer, and it is wrong!" Do you agree? Can you think of situations where simple answers are the very best answers?

Works Cited

Hume, David. *An Enquiry Concerning Human Understanding.* New York: Macmillan, 1955.

Kant, Immanuel. *The Critique of Pure Reason*, trans. N.K. Smith. London: Macmillan, 1963.

Marcel, Gabriel. *Being & Having*, trans. K. Farrer. Boston: Beacon Press, 1951.

————. "On the Ontological Mystery," from *The Philosophy of Existentialism*, trans. M. Harrari. Secaucus, N.J.: Citadel Press, 1973.

Wittgenstein, Ludwig. *Philosophical Investigations*, trans. G.E.M. Anscombe. Oxford: Basil Blackwell, 1968.

————. *Tractatus, Logico-Philosophicus*, trans. D.F. Pears and B.F. McGuiness. London: Routledge & Kegan Paul, 1961.